Udo Kultermann

The New Sculpture

Environments and Assemblages

FREDERICK A. PRAEGER, Publishers
New York · Washington

BOOKS THAT MATTER

Published in the United States of America in 1968
by Frederick A. Praeger, Inc., Publishers
111 Fourth Avenue, New York, N.Y. 10003

Copyright in Tübingen, Germany, by Verlag Ernst Wasmuth, Tübingen, 1967
Translated from the German *Neue Dimensionen der Plastik* by Stanley Baron
English translation copyright in London, England, by Thames and Hudson Ltd, London, 1968

Library of Congress Catalog Card Number: 68-17366

Printed in Germany

CONTENTS

This book is not directed towards one individual achievement in any specific part of the world: neither in Germany, where it was written, nor in Paris, Milan, London, Tokyo, New York or Los Angeles—the centres of contemporary art. It has been written in recognition of various trends and their specific results in these various places, but also attempts to show the interconnections, which are more important today than ever. As in the book 'New Architecture in the World', published in 1965 and since translated into several languages, the theme is world-wide developments and the new interrelatedness in world culture—in this case in the area of the plastic arts and the art of environment.

An undertaking of this sort—from one person's outlook—is bound to be subjective, fragmentary and subject to the particular experiences of that person. And yet it is an attempt, in the present context of artistic developments diffused among all countries, to extract the particular contributions of individual artists from countries with varying cultural traditions.

Any other method of investigating the culture of today is certain to fail, for only with a broad view can the qualitative forces be recognized, only a synoptic approach can make clear the lines of development inherited from their respective traditions. The author's opinions may be arguable in many respects; but his aim has been to work out international standards for the discussion of art in our time.

Contemporary plastic art throughout the world is an artistic language which, though part of a larger context, can be understood and discussed only in terms of its own particular materials: sculpture, relief and constructions resulting from the artist's work with mass, created space, line and colour, pre-existing or new objects. The subtle distinctions of two- and three-dimensional sculpture based on techniques or the genesis of terms have become illusory; they no longer play any role in the present-day situation. The common factor today is the totality of the working process of mass in space.

The techniques transmitted by the traditional plastic arts—forging, casting, carving, soldering and welding—are still used along with the newer methods—collage, body-casting, synthetics, magnetics, electricity and changes of atmospheric pressure. There is no area of human activity which the sculptor cannot take up and use in his work.

The plastic arts, in the widest sense, are a central expression of contemporary art. Whereas the significant changes in the art of fifty years ago took place in the field of painting, the accent has transferred—noticeably since 1950 and quite obviously since 1960—to the field of plastic-spatial art. The search for greater authenticity may have played a part in this.

Numerous painters also use elements of plastic effect in so far as they seek to involve the viewer's space with their materials. Indeed many painters have gone over entirely to the plastic arts. Nor can one overlook the transformation in architecture from the strong, geometric, skeleton form of construction, to dynamic space-forms, ideas of cave-like protectiveness, and plastic forms for living. Our culture is ruled by an ever-increasing tendency towards the plastic-spatial; and this goes hand in hand with an inclination towards synthesis, which runs counter to the long predominant striving for isolation, geometric order and 'appropriate' material.

Certainly the technique, the process of the production of sculpture, is important and —in its place—worth investigation. Yet one diverges more and more from the presentation; the technique or the material themselves already shed some light on the value of the work. The candidness of the work-process has freed the eye for the meaningful character of the work, which one uses (unconsciously, if possible) for magical, symbolic and fetishistic effects. Already in 1937 Carola Giedion-Welcker, in her book 'Moderne Plastik', used a quotation from J.J.Bachofen, 'Only symbols immediately strike all the strings of the human spirit', and referred to the subterranean connection of modern times to the uncomplicated emotions and simple, direct symbols of mythical prehistory. Following the temporary narrowing of the horizon which took place in the area of abstract sculpture governed by doctrinaire ideologies, a freedom of artistic possibilities has now opened up, which can be no more than indicated here. This book seeks to show the quality of contemporary sculpture which has appeared in all countries, with special consideration of the tasks which face the artist today. It will be recognized that certain tasks stand in the foreground while others recede. The much discussed integration of plastic work into the architectonic ensemble, like that of the individual building into the town-planning context, has very rarely produced valid and convincing results. Sculpture oriented towards rooms has had a far stronger development than numerous doctrinaire theories.

The striving for the concrete, however, is no longer confined to the plastic arts. The close relationship of sculpture to music, the dance, theatre and Happenings is also significant. Various sculptors have gone over directly to the dance and Happenings, have produced stage-sets, drawn musical elements into their work, and made films. A more direct approach to reality is also sought by including the factor of time. Live elements and processes are drawn into the work—and indeed not only with the methods of illusion.

After cautious hints in the preceding decades, a new development has also been announced regarding content. The sculptor George Segal recently expressed this in answer to an inquiry: '... an openness of attitude, a willingness to use unfamiliar materials, forms and unorthodox stances in the work produced, an unwillingness to accept standard value judgments, a tendency to probe, act, live, and work with final judgment suspended, an appreciation of the mystery, unknowability, ambiguity of the simplest things.'

A new anti-rationalism in the exceedingly rational use of technical media finds its expression in structures which are complex symbols of new myths. Though no one in our 'enlightened' age might have expected it, ideas such as the magic in things, totem, fetish, ritual and taboo, to which we were uncommitted only a short while ago, are playing a decisive role today. In a way which surprises even ourselves, our reality corresponds to a prehistoric vocabulary.

As early as 9 January 1917, Hugo Ball wrote, 'Self-assertion implies the art of self-transformation. The isolated man seeks to assert himself in unfavourable circumstances; he has to make himself inviolate. Magic is the last refuge of individual self-assertion, perhaps even of the individual.' And a few months later, on 7 May 1917, he made this note: '... aren't we magical eclecticists?'

The signs of a new magic are not, however, retrogressive, nor are they oriented towards pre-technical ideals. On the contrary, artists use the newest of technical innovations much more as a matter of course, use them legitimately in the process of artistic work and thus contribute to the mastery of them. The phenomena of the age of mass media, of electronic energy, of instruments of acceleration, which increasingly surpass the human capacity, have given a new value to the archetypal and primitive. Technology and sorcery, hallucination and precision instruments, the absurdity of subconscious imaginings and the most exact statistical findings, correspond in their results and have become the materials suitable only to our times for coming to terms with reality.

The hierarchy of contents and materials, values and goods, people and states, which prevailed so long out of arrogance and lack of self-confidence, has been conquered. Freedom of choice has also embraced the effects of foreign cultures or our own, past or present; indeed past, present and future are on a level. Idols of the cavemen, fetishes from Africa and Polynesia, masterpieces of antiquity and the Renaissance, but also shop advertisements and television programmes, industrial products and automobile graveyards—everything has become material for the sculptor of today, whether in the sense of taking over the material itself, paraphrasing it, imitating the form, or appropriating it by quotation or violation of its character. The hegemony of the spirit over other forms of human expression is finally overcome, and there has arisen a wholesome frankness and freedom, whose possibilities and laws, frontiers and dangers, still have to be learnt.

In the last few years a transformation has come about in the plastic arts. A new world has been revealed, in which the image of man has reappeared. When Peter Selz put on the exhibition 'New Images of Man' at the Museum of Modern Art, New York, in 1959, a turning-point seemed to be indicated, a new evaluation seemed to be reached of the human image, so long neglected in sculpture and painting.

The arguments presented by Paul Tillich and Peter Selz in their introductions to the catalogue seem now to have been written in clear recognition of this turning-point, and yet they are in fact related to other phenomena and have no bearing at all on the changes which one has apprehended again in entirely different experiences since about 1960. The theologian Tillich interpreted the works of the 1959 exhibition as signs of objectified protest against fate. In his introduction Peter Selz drew the following conclusion with regard to the quite different image of man in the manipulated art of the dictators: 'These images do not indicate the "return to the human figure" or the "new humanism" which the advocates of the academies have longed for, which indeed they and their social-realist counterparts have hopefully proclaimed with great frequency, ever since the rule of the academy was shattered. There is surely no sentimental revival and no cheap self-aggrandizement in these effigies of the disquiet man!'

Following this alienation, as important then as today, from the more or less healthy image of man which still forms the main contingent of art exhibitions or officially sponsored prizes, Selz came to a more precise characterization of the artists included in his exhibition. What he regarded as the factor they had in common was their lack of satisfaction with so-called 'significant form'. With reference to the period in which most of these works had been created, he said of the artists: 'They are perhaps aware of the mechanized barbarism of a time which, notwithstanding Buchenwald and Hiroshima, is engaged in the preparation of even greater violence in which the globe is to be the target.'

Thus Peter Selz outlined the atmosphere of catastrophe in which these artists' works were produced. The sculptors had made their theme the image of man as disturbed, fragmented, dehumanized, manipulated, and almost mechanized. Germaine Richier's 'Bull Fight' shows the body of a man in the shape of a violin, broken up, wounded. The

1 Henry Moore *Reclining Figure* 1963/1964

limbs are formed like sticks, the head has the shape of a half-moon. Related to expressionism and surrealism, this deals with a thematic deformation whose content is the degradation of man. Man can no longer be represented as an intact being. Germaine Richier's 'Le Griffu' (Pl. 3) is a creature halfway between the human and the animal, and 'Batman' anticipates a later mass-idol in a demonic and frightening way. Man and plant were already fused into a single being in Julio Gonzales' 'L'homme cactus' (1939, Pl. 5), and Henry Moore's works of the same period are at one and the same time reclining bodies and ruined landscapes (Pl. 1).

The international competition organized in 1953 for a monument to the unknown political prisoner conformed to this social and artistic situation (Pls. 242 — 245). The theme was the peril of man and his vulnerability to the powers of violence, devastation and chaos.

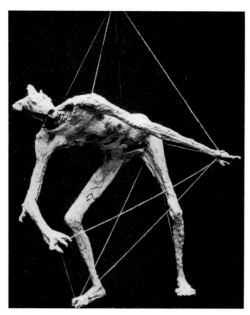

3 Germaine Richier *Le Griffu* 1952

4 Alberto Giacometti *Trois figures II* 1949

Most of the sculptors who took part in the 1953 competition confronted deformed man with a system which threatened or oppressed him: torture machinery, stakes, cages, fences, weapons. In most cases, however, the quality was not up to the demands of the theme.

The First Prize was awarded to the British sculptor, Reg Butler. Most critics mistakenly disparaged his design for being abstract and anti-human (Pl. 242). Butler's piece, which is neither abstract nor anti-human, sought to grasp the anti-human thematically by sculptural means descended from abstraction. His images of destroyed man are called 'Falling Figure', 'Machine', 'St Catherine'. Butler was at that time particularly engaged with the saint on a wheel; torture was a theme of the times. The figure, with mutilated limbs, floats on a barbed wire construction, the head is only suggested, the shin-bones turn into rods. The oppressed man of those years dictated the form.

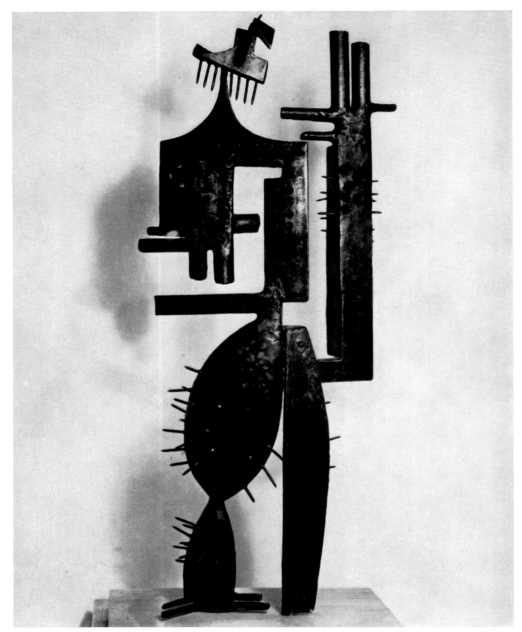

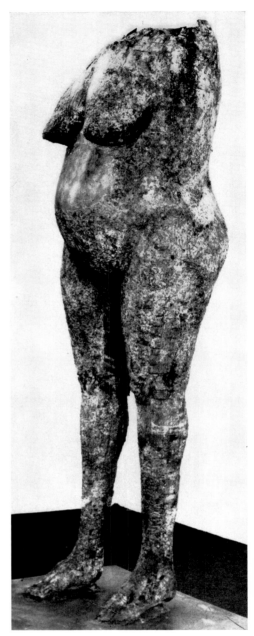

5 Julio Gonzales *L'homme cactus* 1939

6 César *Victoire de Villetaneuse*

In Butler's model for the monument to the unknown political prisoner, this conception, architectonically expressed, attained a universal effect. Significantly, in the course of his work, he reached the point where he left out the originally planned figure of the unknown political prisoner and retained only the architectural form which was reminiscent of the watch-towers of a concentration camp. The reaction against the work was symptomatic: during its exhibition at the Tate Gallery, London, the original model was damaged (Pl. 242).

The image of man is stronger and more convincing in the works produced by Alberto Giacometti who, coming from the surrealist tradition, had found his way to bronze figure work long before 1953. He created a suggestive, indeed hallucinatory, relationship between his elongated, idol-like figures and the surrounding space (Pl. 4).

7 Yves Klein *Portrait Relief Arman* 1962

9 Antoni Gaudí *Degollación de los Santos Inocentes,* Sagrada Familia, Barcelona

10 George Segal *John Chamberlain Working* 1965

Left:
8 George Segal *Robert and Ethel Scull* 1965

In Giacometti's case, too, it is not a question of presenting particular individuals, although the artist used to work daily with models. He has said himself: 'When I tried to create from memory what I had seen, to my horror the statues became thinner and thinner, only when they were very thin did they achieve likeness, yet their dimensions startled me; unflagging, I began over and over again, and in the end, after many months, I was back at the same point.' Here is a kind of obsession which, in the demand for greater accuracy, transforms not only reality, but also the image of man, in a way that is imaginatively experienced by the artist. In 1959 Giacometti answered a critic's query: 'It may be that in all this I am no more than possessed, from causes unknown to me, or compensating for some sort of deficiency.'

Alberto Giacometti was not reacting here only to the question of a critic who had hit upon the basic conditions of his art, but also to the universal situation of his times. For him, artistic creation was the realization of a general failure. 'Artistic success' meant less to him than artistic denial. The themes of the period found their fitting expression.

As in Butler's case, but much more deeply, Giacometti is ruled by the chaos of reality. The annihilation of millions of people on battlefields, in concentration camps and in flight, prevents him too from a lofty elevation of the image of man. Where this has been attempted, the results proved to be unconvincing from the artistic as well as the social and human point of view.

The new image of man has nothing to do with these expressions already mentioned. In works of art since 1960, man confronts us in an entirely different guise: as idealized, stereotyped, intact, authentic, rather than phenomenal, reality. This image is not that of expressionism, surrealism or tachism. Up to Butler, Richier and Giacometti, the image of man was sculpturally translated, communicated according to the imaginative concepts of the artist. It said something metaphorically about what moved the artist, and was related to his temporal situation, his human reality.

The sculpture of an Yves Klein, George Segal, Edward Kienholz or Frank Gallo, takes over the human being—in principle as authentically as possible—from reality, and seeks to let this make its own effect. War and devastation, disintegration, dissolution and deformation are no longer the theme; in fact there is no longer any striving for expression, construction, 'art' in the old sense. This sculpture restricts itself to the existing forms of contemporary people, as they appear on television, in films, advertisements and magazines, particularly in big-city life. The image of man that results from this basic premise, and which in fact again takes the individual as the point of departure while turning him into a generalized stereotype, does not recognize destruction in the same sense as abstract art. Rather it uses the actuality of individual bodily existence, draws on this reality directly and treats it in a documentary fashion for a new artistic effect. The less any of the artist's personal 'shaping' can be perceived in the work, the better; the more the effect is one of an actual manifestation, the better. Something which in itself already exists, ready-made and comprehensive, is used as the total object. Paradoxically the result is an opening up of form, an expansion of the artistic system.

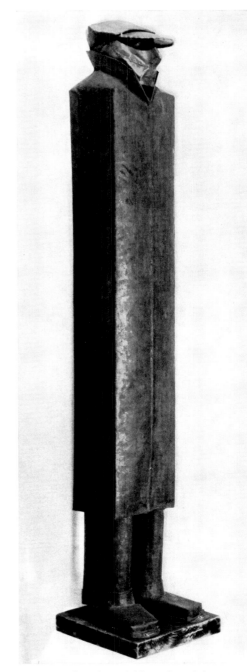

11 Ludvik Durchanek *Homo Derelicto* 1964–1965

Right:
12 Marisol *The Kennedy Family* 1960

13 Marisol *The Party* 1965–1966

14 Edward Kienholz *Barney's Beanery* 1965

Right:
15 Ernest Trova *Study Falling Man* 1966

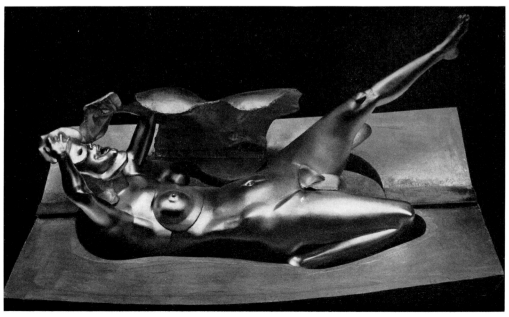

17 Jean Ipoustéguy *La femme au bain* 1966

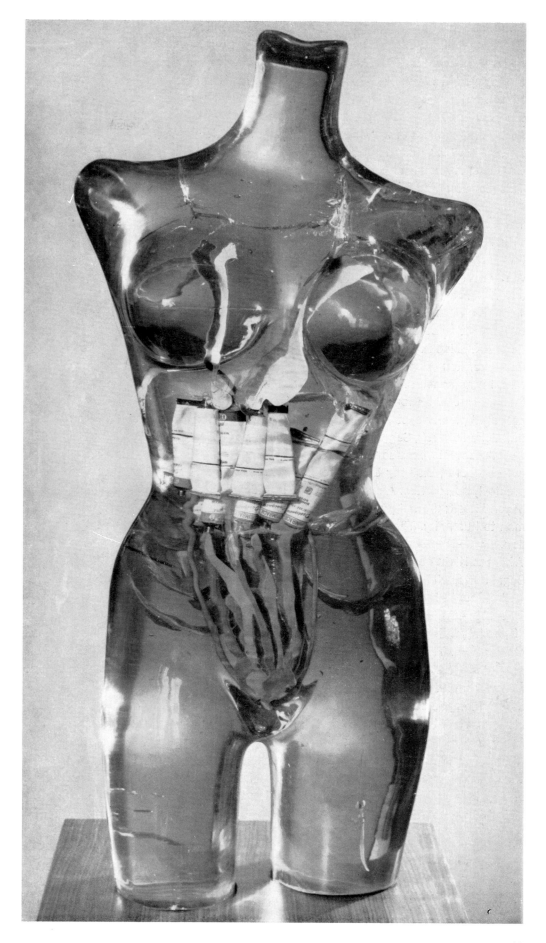

18 Arman *La couleur de mon amour* 1966

The mention of archetypes in view of the new results of contemporary culture has been justified. This becomes clear above all in the new conception of the image of man. In Europe and the United States, the work produced since about 1960, which though varied has moved in the same direction, indicates a new departure. Yves Klein's relief portrait of Arman (1962, Pl. 7) is one of the most persuasive examples of the new concept in Europe. In pursuing the body-printing of blue-painted female nudes on expanses of white paper or canvas, Yves Klein started in 1962 to make plaster casts of his artist friends; of these, the only one he finished, the relief of Arman, was cast in bronze.

This piece shows the artist life size, his arms hanging down and his hands balled into fists. The shins are lacking; the body reaches only as far as the middle of the thighs. The head is raised and he gazes into the distance. The finished casting was painted with Yves Klein's characteristic blue and placed in front of a golden relief surface. In this cast taken from an actual nude body, the artist was still working within the framework of Western tradition, and yet, by the use of his two favourite colours, he created a work with a quite new, unsuspected intensity of radiance.

The directness of the cast, to which nothing was added except colour — something which used to be commonly understood in creative interpretation in the field of plastic art—the lack of anything problematic or symbolic, the lack of any expression, the unadulterated effect of actual corporeality, and the blue and gold, make this sculpture, in the sense of a new art-less art, a key work. A remarkable prototype for this technique can be found in the work of the Catalan architect, Antonio Gaudí, who prepared plaster casts of living people and animals for the plastic decoration of his unfinished church, Sagrada Familia, in Barcelona (Pl. 9).

Segal's sculptures also proceed from real people, plastically established figures whose bodies, clothing and surroundings are not reproduced, but documented as precisely as possible. A moment in time is endowed with something that operates far beyond itself; the unique man taken as the subject preserves something that is common to humanity. The objectivity of the figures in their surroundings stirs meditation.

Whereas Klein colours the bodies of his portrait-reliefs with his typical blue, George Segal leaves all his figures the colour of plaster, and the objects which indicate their environment—the automobile, the work of art by Chamberlain, the bar, the pinball machines—he leaves in the colours these objects normally have. Segal first bandages his models with cloth wrappings, which are soaked in a durable, industrially produced plaster-bath. Then the casting is undertaken in various phases, during which it is possible to make slight changes in the models' attitudes, which are meant to appear as commonplace, as casual, as 'real' as possible.

Segal's composition of 1965, 'John Chamberlain Working' (Pl. 10), shows the artist in his work-clothes busy at one of his projects. It is iconographically interesting that Segal, as well as Yves Klein, who had started further portraits of Martial Raysse and Claude Pascal, uses his artist friends as models, as was usual in the age of romanticism, more than a century and a half ago. This is not the only analogy to artistic modes of the nineteenth century, which is also being studied anew and re-evaluated by art historians.

19 Ivor Abrahams *The Huntress* 1963–1966

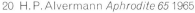

20 H. P. Alvermann *Aphrodite 65* 1965

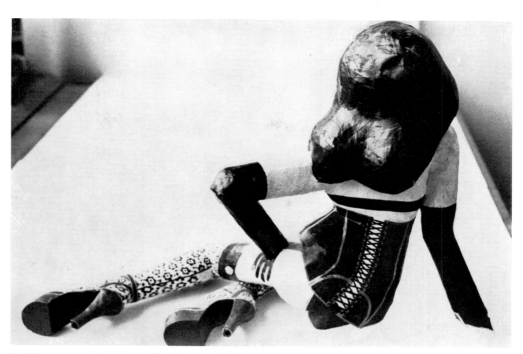

21 Michael John Davidson *Viva Maria* 1967

22 Michael John Davidson *Big Stripper* 1967

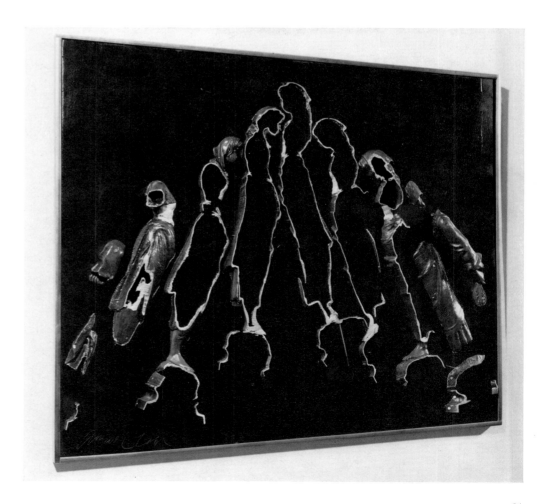

23 Arman *La jeune fille pauvre* 1962

Right:
25 Mario Ceroli *Il Mister* 1965

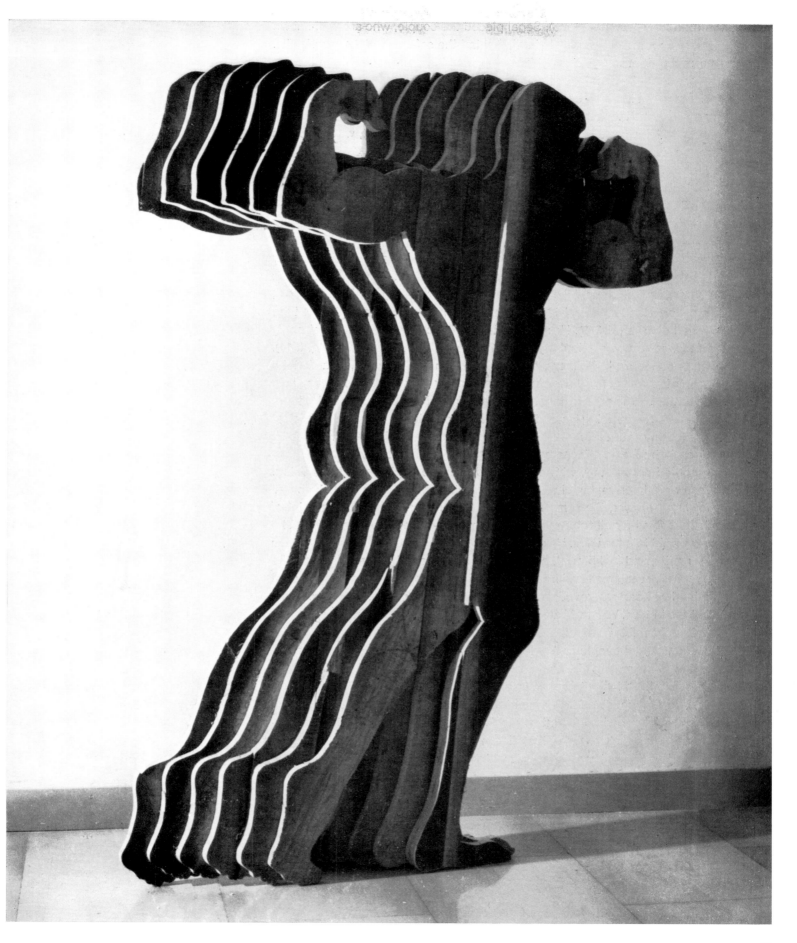

In 'Robert and Ethel Scull' (1965, Pl. 8), Segal placed the couple, who are well-known art collectors, in a room: Robert Scull stands behind the sofa on which his wife sits. She wears a real pair of sunglasses which intensifies the contrast between the figures, made unreal-real by their lack of colour, and their commonplace surroundings. The fixing of a moment in time plays a further important role: the human-spatial relationship is preserved 'to the life', fortuitous and unique. Thus the sculptor once again fulfils functions which were already ascribed to him in ancient Egypt, where he was called 'preserver of life'.

In more recent works, such as 'Legend of Lot' (1966), Segal has gone from his commonplace subjects to pre-existing legends, in which a defined theme guides both the artist's production and its effect on the viewer. In 1966, in an exhibition at the Sidney Janis Gallery in New York, Segal had the Lot text from the Bible hung behind the sculpture.

The example of these methods attracted Edward Kienholz, whose work is of pioneer importance to the art situation on the West Coast of the United States. In part he has used Segal's casting technique. Like Yves Klein, however, and in contrast to Segal, who usually casts clothed models, Kienholz starts with nude castings, which he then dresses with real clothes (Pl. 358). He represents the environment even more strongly than Segal does, as shown particularly in his 1965 work, 'Barney's Beanery' (Pl. 14). Kienholz has fixed Barney's Beanery, an artists' bar in Los Angeles, at a definite date in 1964; this is clearly established through a number of newspapers on a rack at the entrance to the bar. The room, together with the people who happen to be there by chance (they are reduced in size, as the whole composition is two-thirds of actual size), is portrayed in casts and real fragments as an ensemble. The work makes its effect only as a whole; the details can be understood only in their context.

Man is represented here bodily, with clothes and with the implements he is using. Only the heads have been replaced with clocks, clocks of the most varied kinds and form, all showing, however, the same time: 10.10. This instant, chosen as a point of departure, is thus fixed for all future time as if in a three-dimensional snapshot. The viewer can step right into the work. He can sit down next to one of the figures who was once there in reality, and feel himself a part of this spatial and human milieu. All the senses are aroused, even smell and hearing: a television broadcast is on, the special odour of the bar has been preserved, and one can order drinks which were ordinarily being drunk there in 1964. What will a person feel in 50, 100, 300 years from now, when he steps into this ensemble?

The artist deals with real people and real spatial contexts. These are actual and not interpreted; it is not a matter of transformation, but an attempt to document. This work is the present, itself including of course both past and future. The moment preserved is 10.10 on 18 August 1964. Barney himself, owner of the bar, the only figure whose head has not been changed into a clock, reads the Los Angeles Herald-Examiner. The headline reads, 'Children Kill Children in Vietnam Riots'.

In Kienholz's works, with their new concepts which have little to do with art in the old sense, or even with pop art, dimensions have been disclosed which seem to be without any tradition at all. Yet it may not be wrong to presume that the after-effects of the Spanish heritage in Los Angeles and neighbouring Mexico—one thinks of the spatial naturalism and the use of real clothing in Spanish baroque sculpture—are appearing afresh.

Many artists, like Kienholz, have contributed to a new conception of the image of man. In the United States, for example, William King and his view of man as raw data should be mentioned. Sculptors such as Manuel Neri, Ludvik Durchanek (Pl. 11) and Anne Arnold start from similar assumptions. But most important of all in

this context is Marisol Escobar, who comes from Venezuela. Under the influence of her teacher, William King, who already in 1955 in his work 'Marisol' (Pl. 53) sought an interweaving of space and symbol, she has tried to achieve more intense effects through authenticity. In 1963 she showed John Wayne shooting from a hobby-horse; his face is indicated by a photograph. In her work 'The Kennedy Family' (Pl. 12), produced in 1960, she placed together three stele-like wooden blocks and personalized them with applied photographs. The largest of the blocks is identified as John F. Kennedy—at that time President—by photographic details of his mouth, eyes and nose. The somewhat smaller block on his right is characterized as a female by two round shapes at breast-height, and identified by the physiognomy of Jacqueline Kennedy. Standing on his left is another smaller block, with a child's head on it, representing the Kennedys' elder child; the little block lying across the mother's lap is their younger child as a baby. In this work composed of varied materials, descriptive symbols and documents are combined in a concept which points beyond them, and this constitutes the special effect, touching the field of magic, of this type of work. In 'The Bathers' (1961–2), made of painted wood and plaster, Marisol built up wooden forms in the simplified shape of human bodies in front of a nondescript wall, and applied to them recognizable objects which give the effect of painting.

From then on Marisol has taken a greater interest in spatial relations. These efforts culminate in the large work 'The Party', of 1965–6 (Pl. 13). Fifteen life-size figures of stele-like character stand in a room. The heads all carry photographic portraits or casts of the artist's face. That social institution which looms so large in the United States—the 'party'—is realized in figures who stand in the room, near but unrelated to one another, bound up within themselves, indeed isolated while at the same time identified with one another through the recurring self-portrait. Thus they form a magical company whose grouping has a ceremonial character. The figures, which are differentiated by extravagant dresses, coiffures, hats and mimed gestures, are not conceived as people who once existed, but consciously offered as types, as embodiments of forms of behaviour. Even some of the waiters carrying trays and glasses bear multiple reproductions of the artist's face. The unconnected relationship of the parts of the ensemble forms the real content of this environmental sculpture, the party.

Again quite different is the image of man in artists like Robert Cremean and Ernest Trova. For several years, Trova has made the so-called 'Falling Man' his basic theme (Pls. 15 and 52). His polished metal castings show anonymous figures, sexless, armless and faceless, who possess no individuality. Placed in specific surroundings, they embody the technified image of contemporary man. Trova's sculptures have correctly been called depersonalized figures. In these works man partially approaches the machine, or coalesces with it. In the 'Wheel-Man' of 1965, man is identified with the instrument quite differently from the way Butler or Paolozzi attempted this some years earlier. The connection of man and automobile has been indicated by a number of artists: Charles Frazier (Pl. 130), Marisol, Salvatore Scarpitta (Pl. 131), Edward Kienholz (Pls. 129 and IV). In 'Car-Man' of 1966, Trova provided a Falling Man with four wheels, thus identifying person and machine. Trova's more recent industrial art, also tending towards larger spatial contexts, uses production conditions and the emotional clichés of our society. 'Study Falling Man' (Pl. 15) inserts the figure into a system of two glass cases linked together.

Most of the European sculptors, such as Arman (Pls. 18 and 23), Paul van Hoeydonck (Pl. 97), Ivor Abrahams (Pl. 19), Jean Ipoustéguy (Pl. 17) and H.P. Alvermann (Pl. 20), adhere to an abbreviated, i.e., surrealistically alienated, presentation of man. This conception is rare among the Americans. But European sculptors are also aware of the cliché image of man as sound and intact. The concept expressed in the work of the Italian, Mario Ceroli, is of man as a serial type. Ceroli takes his figuration either from reality, e. g., by placing the silhouettes of models in a row, or from artistic tradition. This is the basis of his 'L'uomo di Leonardo' (1964, Pl. 26) as well as other recent works, in which Leonardo da Vinci's illustration of human proportions—enlarged and transferred onto wood—appears repeatedly. Another work of Ceroli's shows the reversed silhouette of Venus (from Botticelli's 'Birth of Venus' in the Uffizi, Pl. 24), enlarged and cut out of wood, in seven rows, one behind the other. The result is a kind of moving-picture, modelled on photo-series and films.

In 'The Mister' (1965, Pl. 25), Ceroli used the same technique on a male model, showing the ideal of the masses as an advertisement for body-building, which has such a strong effect on many people. Here too the meaning is not that of an individual participating in the Mr Universe contest, but the mass image of an idol, a star. This phantom, which exercises a life-stimulating effect on the unsuspecting masses, is a reality.

In Ceroli's work of the last few years, as in the work of American artists, one can see a turning towards larger spatial contexts. His 'Cassa Sistina' of 1966 (Pl. 27), a simple wooden hut, is furnished inside with folding silhouettes of male and female nudes which can be arranged at will. Ceroli has created in this way a room entirely determined by the human figure, for these wooden silhouettes, copied from the shadows of real people, remain recognizable as human figures; at the same time they produce a multiple and changeable composite picture which permits constantly new constellations. A person can enter, take part in this shadow-reality, and alter it. The external bodily appearance of man is schematized either in form or in content, i.e., the images are taken either from the cliché reality of today, or from those images in past art which familiarity has made into clichés. In either case the objects are ready-made; psychology no longer plays any role or has moved into a new realm.

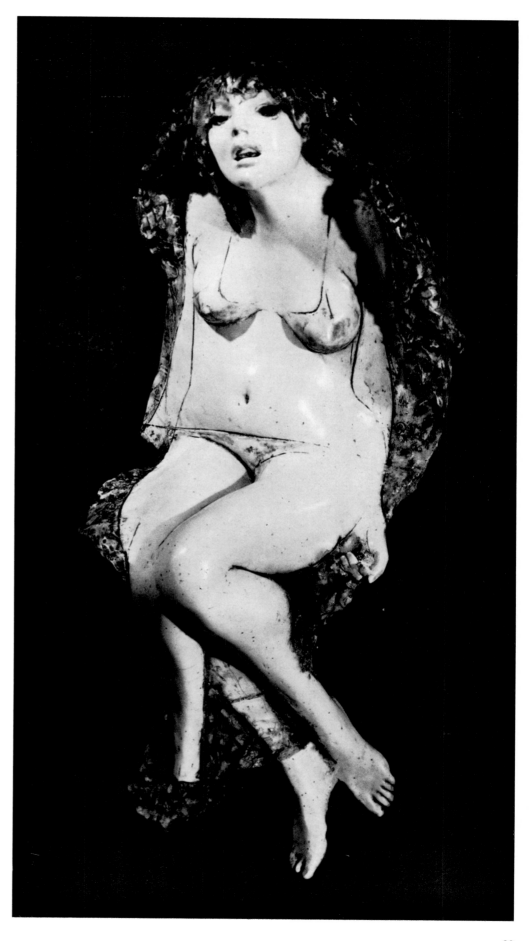

29 Frank Gallo *Love Object* 1966

The most radical expression of this new viewpoint is the work 'China' of 1967, in which the subject is the serried ranks of a troop-concentration. The schematized silhouettes of figures are a faceless crowd, but a few of them are singled out by means of individualized profiles. A comparison with real mass-demonstrations, in which individuals are like instruments in the hands of a choreographer, makes the authenticity of this sort of composition meaningful. For instance in 1965 thousands of schoolchildren in the Peking Stadium arranged themselves with coloured cardboard boxes so as to form gigantic propagandistic pictures of five Freedom Fighters. The theme and material of these compositions is manipulated man. The movable pictures and reliefs of Thomas Bayrle, alluding to the realities of American advertisements, are concerned with the same theme. The effort to produce on the individual's wish-projection an effect as close to the clichés of reality, as documentary and as direct as possible, is strongly marked in the work of Frank Gallo (Pl. 28). Gallo has concentrated basically on female nudes, which he makes, under life size, out of plastics, and whose specific effect rests on their direct resemblance to nature. In his 'Love Object' (1966, Pl. 29), the factors of female attraction are emphasized: the smoothness of the skin, the open mouth, the glance from eyes with long lashes. The true-to-life imitation of the pin-up's pose gives this work its special effect.

The authenticity of this composition lies in its intense titillation, which is provided again and again in innumerable magazines, in a great deal of publicity and in the mass media. This new naturalism which, as in the case of Segal or Yves Klein, uses the particular person only for the purpose of creating something more general or archetypal, reminds one of the sculpture of Max Klinger or the paintings of Fernand Khnopff and Félicien Rops.

30 Mauro Kunst *Bones* 1965

31 Robert Graham *Untitled* 1966

32 Robert Graham *Untitled* 1966

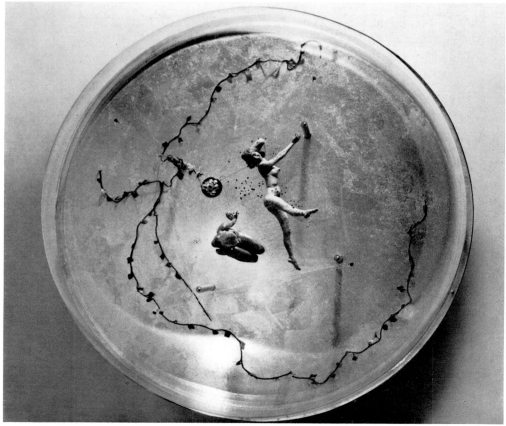

33 Robert Graham *Untitled* 1966

34 Robert Graham *Untitled* 1966

Gallo has also created portraits in the same technique. In some he has reached back to an early Renaissance form of bust-portrait. Though unmistakably contemporary in type and bearing, these portraits, in their reminiscences of past art-forms, exert something of the charm and freshness of a Donatello, Desiderio da Settignano or Luca della Robbia.

The prefabricated clichés of reality can be used even more intensively as the themes of plastic art. It is the world of mass media that Nicholas Munro and Red Grooms show in their work. For instance in 'Dancers' (1966), Munro presents a dancing couple who seem to be taken from a television entertainment programme. In 'Hollywood (Jean Harlow)', Red Grooms has plastically reproduced a scene from a film: the legendary star lies on a semicircular couch, a man in a black suit stands in front of her. The subject of the scene is the portrait of an idol, not of the person Jean Harlow herself. The technique suits the artificial world of make-believe—the entertainment produced for a mass public.

The California sculptress, Jann Haworth, also uses ready-made clichés; but she goes even further with this technique, using cloth and hair in her search for the authenticity of the fabricated. In this respect her 'Surfer' of 1965 goes beyond her earlier work. Jann Haworth (daughter of a film-producer) always relates her themes to the motion-picture language of our times, whose unreality has become more real than reality.

Robert Graham *Untitled* 1967

35 Robert Graham *Untitled* 1966

The clichés of American history (i.e., the pseudo-facts of history books) are the subject of Alex Katz's work. In his relief 'American Flag and Soldiers – Boat – River', he combines painted cut-out figures in the style of stage-set clichés. Katz has also created actual stage-sets.

The sculptors' efforts to get hold of pre-existing things and mass clichés have led even to montages of old works of art. Instead of television idols or historical personalities, Jaak Frenken uses Gothic madonnas or medieval reliefs; they are the materials for a new work of art, which accepts the effectiveness of the ready-made. Neiman uses nude photographs for his plastically transformed montages (Pl. 368).

The sculptor Robert Graham sets his realistically conceived figures or figure-groups under plexiglas domes or cases. The glass covering gives one a view of female and male nudes, landscapes and objects. These figurations always seem to exist independently of the viewer, although this is an entirely calculated effect, particularly through an extremely cultivated interplay of colours. The significance of these works is determined by a new integration of colour and space. One of them contains a group of sunbathers, men and women lying, sitting, standing, obviously absorbed in conversation (Pl. 34). A part of the effect—as in the paintings and reliefs of Tom Wesselmann—is in the charm of the juxtaposition on the bodies of tanned portions and the untanned patterns left by pieces of clothing.

38 Alain Jacquet *La source* 1965

Another work of Graham's shows three naked women under a shower (Pl. 35). The watery ground is reproduced by means of a mirror, which reflects not only the figures but also the construction of the three showers, a plastic curtain, plants and bushes. Under another glass dome, inside which a flowering branch hangs down, a female figure, wearing only a brassiere, is climbing a ladder (Pl. 32).

39 *Yayoi Kusama on Phallic Sofa* 1962

Graham's work, using the allure of pin-ups in the same manner as the paintings of Mel Ramos do, is mainly concerned with representations as commercialized in mass society. But more important is the colouristic charm of his constructions, in which the miniature environment is defined by the colours and the viewer's distance. The seclusion of the space and figures presented under the plastic dome—this appears also, though quite differently worked out, in Mauro Kunst's 'Bones' of 1965 (Pl. 30)—creates relations of colour and space which curiously transform the subject-matter. The result is a spatial aloofness by means of which the clarity of view is not disturbed, while the figures remain untouchable. The quasi-eroticism of the entertainment industry, the nude beaches and Playboy Clubs, are artistically transposed without any recourse to paraphrase, translation or metamorphosis. The glass domes, isolating and revealing simultaneously, are the integrating components of these works.

The new corporeality, which corresponds to our present consciousness of the body, is expressed in the commercial mass media in the same way as in the philosophy of Heidegger, Sartre and Merleau-Ponty. For Merleau-Ponty, Being-Alive, Being-Human, Being-in-the-World and Being-in-Truth are identical terms. The thing-ness of the human body has been discovered in recent literature too (e.g., Robbe-Grillet). This is most strongly demonstrated, however, in the new dance and ballet, which use the body in ways quite different from only a few years ago—as expressive material.

41 Piero Manzoni *Scultura vivente* 1961

42 Niki de Saint Phalle *Hon* 1966

A number of sculptors have drawn far-reaching conclusions from this. In Robert Whitman's so-called 'cinema-sculpture', a nude model moves under a shower behind a plastic screen. The body of a living person is here the sole and ultimate theme, no longer in any form of interpretation, but actual. The model accentuated in Whitman's demonstration by means of the screen and the dark fluid used in place of soap, is in the tradition of the eternal effort to raise man himself into a work of art, as Novalis called for in his romantic philosophy.

Like Whitman, Elio Marchegiani used a nude model in his 'Venus' of 1965 (Pls. 36 and 37). The nude stands in a plexiglas case and is photographed in various positions. The glass surfaces cause distortions which give an effect of alienation to the body.

The next steps from these concepts lead naturally to the breaching of all frontiers towards pantomime, dance, theatre and Happenings, in which an even more direct approach to reality is also sought. The living should be incorporated, not with the methods of illusion, but as reality. Yves Klein's body-printing of female nudes with blue paint was a first example of these new efforts; and so was Piero Manzoni's female

43 Niki de Saint Phalle *Hon* 1966

nude signatures. Manzoni's 'Scultura Vivente' of 1961 (Pl. 41), a plain wooden pedestal with two footprints, makes available a device by which anyone can make his own figures.

Alain Jacquet photographed a nude in the pose of Ingres' famous painting, 'La Source', equipped it mainly for ironic effect with accessories contemporary with the neo-Classical master, and transferred the resulting colour photograph onto a plastic floating figure (Pl. 38). The wrapped nudes of Christo and Höke belong in this context, as well as Yayoi Kusama's practice of using her own image as part of her sculpture (Pl. 39); the Happenings of Otto Mühl, which use bodies and body combinations as 'material action' (Pl. 40); the self-painting of Günter Brus and further Happenings in Osaka, Edinburgh, Paris, New York and Prague, which include naked participants as an element of the demonstration. In such productions man is seen not as man, but as body. Otto Mühl has written: 'The bodies, things, which we ordinarily consider for our use and value as such, are decharacterized of their utility through being used as material' (Pl. 40).

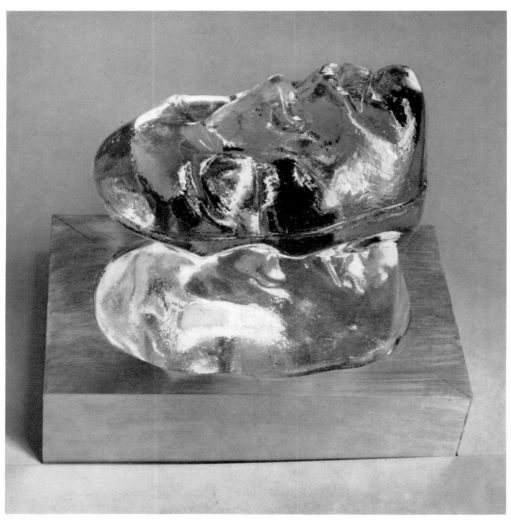

45 Marisol *Kiss* 1966

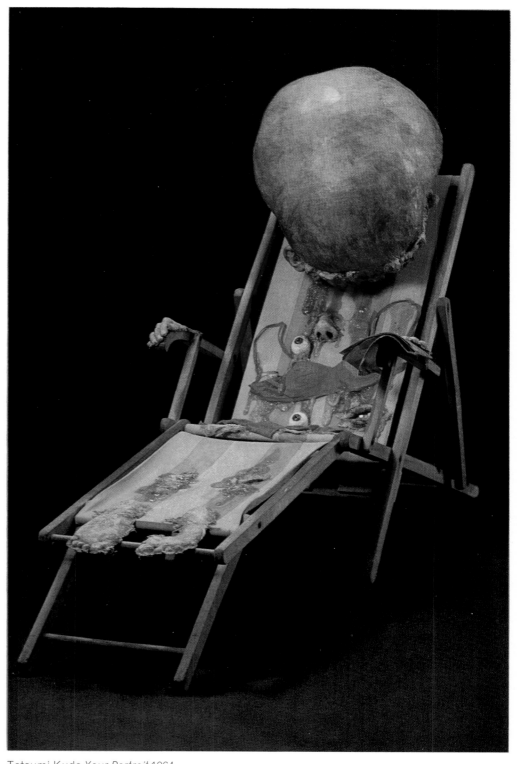

Tetsumi Kudo *Your Portrait* 1964

Even in 1917 Hugo Ball recognized that 'The final result of individualism is magic...' Yves Klein's anthropometries have the same ritual effect as cave-drawings. Segal's shadow-figures in bars, bedrooms or shops are witnesses to our world, isolated even when they are presented in groups, resting in themselves. They bring to mind Tetsumi Kudo's quotations of 'white shadows', which the Hiroshima victims left on walls, as well as the casts taken from depressions left by those who died at Pompeii and Herculaneum. Death and survival, time and space, the pre-experience of humanity, are suggested in these documents of our banal and unmysterious world.

It is not far from this to being obsessed by objects and to a new realization of mythical and magical powers in modern sculpture. Objects you can step into, changeable forms, objects of worship and use—everything can be sculpture in our times. Paul Harris has made figures out of cloth, who dwell in environments also made entirely out of cloth. Subsequent to her colourful cloth dolls, 'Nanas' (Pl. 46), Niki de St Phalle collaborated with Tinguely and Ultfedt in 1966 in making the large 'Hon' (Pls. 42 and 43) in Stockholm: an edifice in a woman's shape which spectators can walk through. One steps into the form of a person, rather as suggested by a recent science fiction story, in which miniaturized researchers are introduced into the blood-stream of a human body.

46 Niki de Saint Phalle *Benedicte* 1965

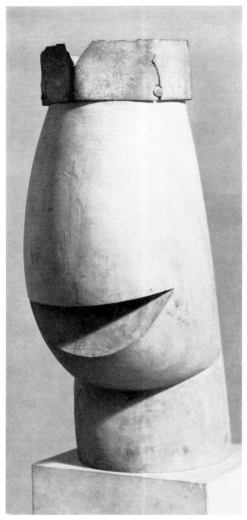

47 Constantin Brancusi *Chieftain* 1925   48 Eduardo Paolozzi *Man with Wheel* 1956   49 Karel Nepraś *Hlava* 1964

Even in the great age of the capitalists, the 1880s, one liked to enter enormous figure monuments, e.g., the Statue of Liberty in New York or the Hermanns monument in Teutoburger Wald. It was a means by which a person experienced the immediate connection between limited and open space, which had got lost in the preceding decades of recent art. New ritual powers, for the most part unintelligible but nevertheless effective, are thus activated. They still elude conventional art criticism and demand new categories of judgment.

Long forgotten and now revived visions of the inner and outer worlds of human potentialities have been unlocked again and have lifted to consciousness regions in the understanding of man and the world which had previously been suppressed. The new image of man plays a decisive, indeed a programmatic role, in the stereotypes of the human form. It is not a distorted, crippled, cramped and deformed image of man that confronts us here, but an idol-like enhanced image, which nevertheless paradoxically evokes rejection. This rejection applies only in art, not in the mass media, advertising or commercialized sport. One may regard the images of man in art this way or that, one may want to rise above them or to close one's eyes before them, but one cannot shove them aside, let alone try to change them. They manifest the human image in a period of electronic energy, space-travel, hidden persuasion, and exercise an entirely new fascination.

Parts of the body also can be made the direct subject-matter of art and, as in the past, be endowed with ritualistic function. Nowadays the head becomes not only a portrait, but also an emblem, and then a depersonalized form. Brancusi still used the head as the personification of forces and powers that go beyond the meaning of the particular individual. In this connection his 'Chieftain' (Pl. 47) of 1925 is a key example. In 'Mechanical Head' of 1918, a 'ready-made' constructed with pre-existing details, Raoul Hausmann incorporated colour, volume and technical devices without losing the basic recognizable shape of a head. Already in 1911, Boccioni tried in his 'Fusion of a Head and a Window' to achieve a union of heterogeneous effects. In a quite different way Dali's 'Head of Dante' (1965, Pl. 50) goes directly from the naturalistic features of a portrait of Dante and produces a surrealistic metamorphosis by replacing the crown of laurel with spoons. Eduardo Paolozzi (Pl. 48) and Karel Nepras (Pl. 49) dissolve the head's shape into ravelled ropes and fragments.

Only through a reconstitution based on ready-made clichés, an arrangement of human symbols taken over from the manipulated mass media, did a new image of man develop. Now it is extensively de-individualized, i.e., it approaches specific individual beings only through designations. William King's portrait of Marisol (1955, Pl. 53) is an example of this—or Harold Tovish's 'Vortex' of 1966 (Pl. 51) and Frank Gallo's 'Head of a Fighter' (Pl. 54). This de-personalizing is carried to its extreme in the heads of Trova's 'Falling Figures' (Pl. 52), which retain only the shapes, without any closer characterization.

Double forms, which make their theme the confrontation of two heads, have appeared in the last few years. In 'Double Heads' of 1965, Ruth Francken represents two death's-heads; Marisol's 'Kiss' of 1965 (Pl. 45) consists of glass casts of her own head joined together; Kudo's 'L'Amour' of 1964 (Pl. 44) reproduces a basic human situation—the union of the sexes—which differ distinctly from earlier interpretations of exactly the same theme, as for instance by the art nouveau artists.

50 Salvador Dali *Head of Dante* 1965

51 Harold Tovish *Vortex* 1966

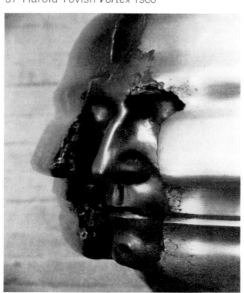

52 Ernest Trova *Study Falling Man* 1965

As in prehistoric art, the human hand has become a particular symbol of reality and significance. The arm reliquaries of the Middle Ages were not just symbols, but real receptacles whose contents were worshipped. The hand of God, the hand as symbol of entry and readiness to make peace, has long played an effective role, even in the post-medieval period. Rodin dealt with this theme frequently. Carl Milles, influenced by Rodin, executed the monumental 'Man in the Hand of God' in Stockholm-Lidingö. Also, Le Corbusier's monument of an open hand in Chandigarh (Pl. 56) unmistakably has this symbolic character transmitted from the past. The hand of Giacometti, however, has a ritual effect in a new sense. Maria Papas' 'Hand of Oedipus' (1965, Pl. 55) shows a hand which is at the same time formed like a face; one can recognize eyes and a nose on the back. But this is still a metamorphosis within the concept of surrealism.

Alik Cavaliere's bronze statue 'The Hand and the Rose' (1965, Pl. 58) evokes a variety of associations on a new plane: elements of sentimental postcards, graveyard sculpture and plant still-lifes.

In 'Le Pouce de César' (1965, Pl. 57), César went even further, isolating his thumb and making it the theme of a plastic work. Robert Hansen's 'Mudra No. 2' shows the hand as a human body: a face appears on the middle finger and the fingernails are formed like hands. This vision of the part in the whole and the whole in the part has its origins in Asia. In fact Hansen was decisively influenced by Hindu ideas during his stay in India. On the other hand Stephen van Huene, in his sculpture 'The Hand' of 1964—the materials are leather and wood—approaches the medieval forms of arm reliquaries. Jim Dine's arms and hands (Pl. 59), growing out of steles, have a direct ritual effect which defies solution.

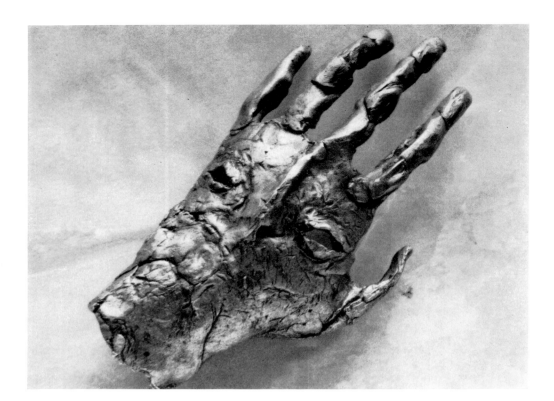

56 Le Corbusier *La main ouverte* 1964

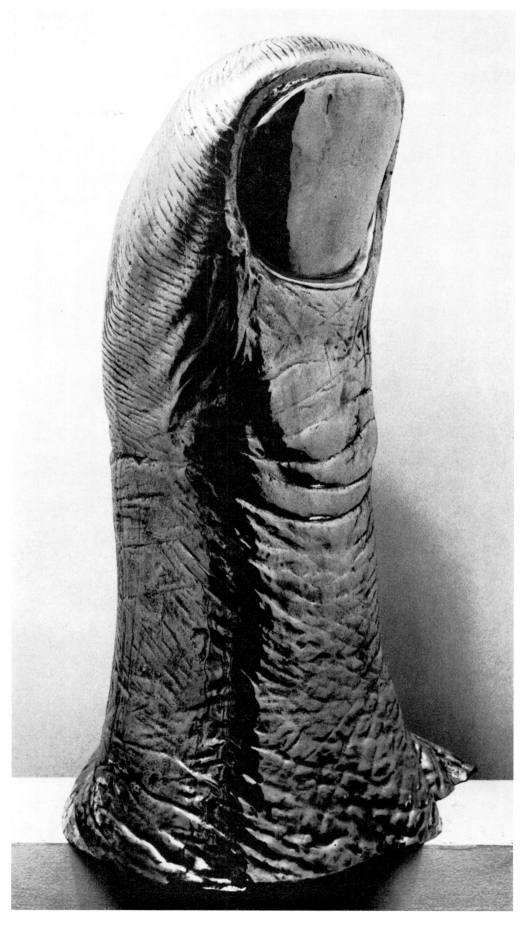

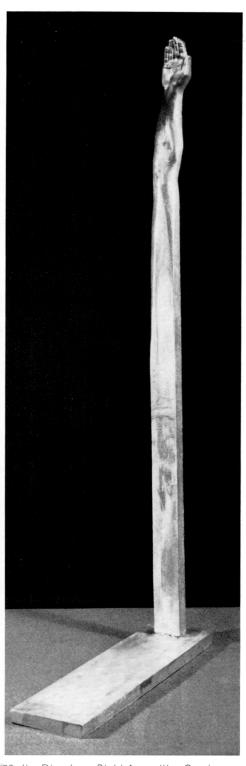

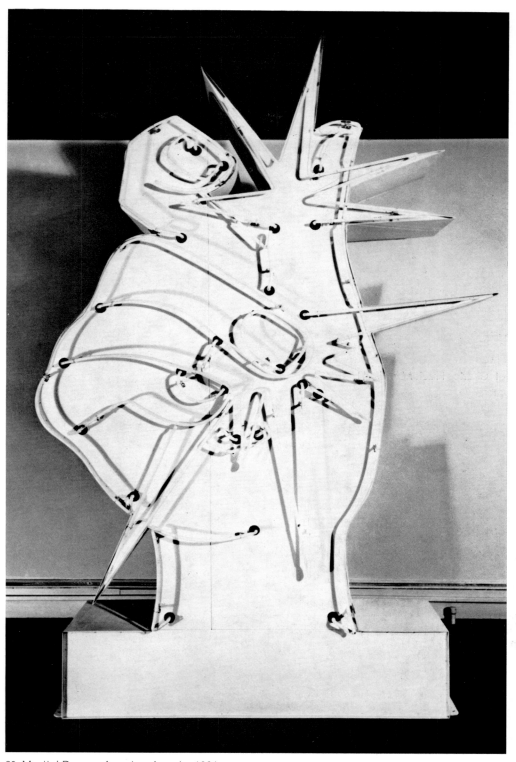

59 Jim Dine *Long Right Arm with a Candy Apple Hand* 1965

60 Martial Raysse *America, America* 1964

Left:
58 Alik Cavaliere *La main et la rose* 1965

For his neon construction 'America, America' of 1964 (Pl. 60), Martial Raysse used the torch-bearing arm of the Statue of Liberty, that oversized allegory of the capitalist 1880s which stands for a symbol of the United States. The hand, as a ready-made form, takes on a new intensity of meaning by its isolation and change of scale. Raysse has taken the light of freedom, allegorically represented in the original, and has made it a real light.

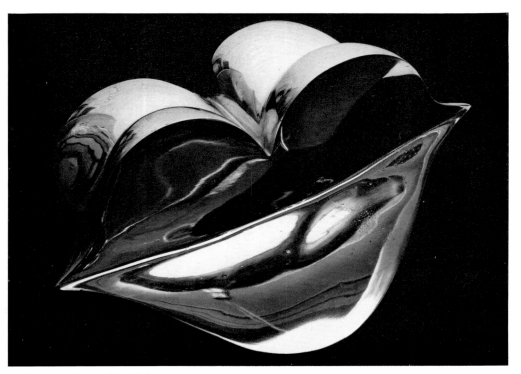

61 Charles Frazier *Untitled* 1965

62 Charles Frazier *Untitled* 1965

63 Pino Pascali *Le labbra rosse* 1964

65 Tetsumi Kudo *For Your Living-Room. For Nostalgic Purposes* 1965

66 Tomio Miki *Untitled* 1965

Other parts of the body are also isolated and become, in the new sense, the subject of sculpture. Here again the Dada-ists and surrealists laid the ground. In his picture 'Observatory Time – The Lovers' (1930–2), Man Ray set a huge mouth against the evening sky. In 1952 Lynn Chadwick made the spiritual eye the theme of a monumental sculpture; its metaphorical treatment is different from the methods he now uses. Only a few years later Jasper Johns, in his 'Targets with Plaster Casts' (1955, Pl. 67), incorporated direct casts of individual parts of the body into a pictorial composition and laid the foundation for a new development. In the boxes which he attached to the upper frame of his large shooting targets, the functions of the body are indicated by nose and mouth, hand, nipples and ears. The Japanese artist Tomio Miki has made ears in all sizes and shapes the theme of his aluminium reliefs (Pl. 66) and has thus gained a basic form for ever new variations. Charles Frazier enlarges lips, isolates them, sets them on pedestals or lets them grow out of spheres (Pls. 61, 62 and 64). The erotic, suggestive effect of the mouth is expressed in Pino Pascali's 'Red Lips' (1964, Pl. 63), as in the paintings of Tom Wesselmann or Peter Stämpfli. In 'Viva Sweet Love' (1964), Charles Frazier assembled primary and secondary female sex indications into one symbol; and in 'For Your Living Room' or 'For Nostalgic Purposes' (1965–6, Pl. 65), Tetsumi Kudo arranged phalluses in bird-cages and thus emphasized a significance thoroughly familiar in prehistory as well as in many non-European cultures.

67 Jasper Johns *Target with Plaster Casts* 1955

ANIMAL SCULPTURE

The representation of animals, like that of man, was one of the favourite themes in the sculpture of the past. A great menagerie, filling innumerable rooms in the museums of present-day Rome, has come down to us from Roman antiquity. In the eighteenth (Pl. 68) and nineteenth centuries too (Barye, Gaul and Hildebrand), this subject occupied sculptors again and finally dominated the work of a painter like Franz Marc. But the first to lead the subject from sheer illustration towards a symbolism beyond the individual animal, were Constantin Brancusi, Pablo Picasso, Raymond Duchamp-Villon and Julio Gonzales. Brancusi's archetypes reach into the magical, e.g., his 'Fish' (1925) or Seal' (1943), which significantly bears the additional title, 'The Wonder', the series of cocks, penguins (Pl. 71) and those unique birds in which the sculpture of the first half of the twentieth century culminated. The image of the bird taking flight was in general one of the central motifs of the new sculpture—an unmistakable expression of the secret longing of the period. For example, bird symbols are uppermost in the work of Max Ernst. They received a monumental treatment in Antoine Pevsner's 'Flight of a Bird' in 1955.

Marcel Duchamp-Villon's representation of the horse became a key work. In his larger pieces, which exist in several versions (1914), he was concerned with the movement of animals, the mechanism of the physiological. Carola Giedion-Welcker wrote of these works: 'Bodily function and rhythm seem to be plastically dissected, so that the naturalistic organism—horse—is utterly extinguished by making the energetic principle prominent.' As early as 1912–13 Boccioni had already created a piece entitled 'Horse and Houses', in which he tried to represent the galloping motion.

Picasso used prefabricated everyday materials for his 'Bull's Head' of 1943 (Pl. 70). He combined the handle-bar and saddle of a bicycle into a magical image of direct reality. The exorcising power of the artistic imagination transformed the ready-made, industrially produced parts of a used bicycle, with their interrelation and their uniqueness. It is noticeable that children fail to react — unlike adults bound by reason — to the constituent parts of the work; they recognize at first sight the animal imagined by the artist. Later works of Picasso ('Monkey and the Baby' of 1952, 'Goat' of 1950, Pl. 69) also include a great number of animal sculptures.

Surrealist art drew on animals for its themes. Miró's 'Objet Poétique' of 1936, for example, consists of a stuffed bird, a man's hat and a woman's leg. The animal image is programmatically used in the surrealist sense in the works of Meret Oppenheim, particularly 'Squirrel' (1960). During the Second World War and after, the subjects of dissolution and amorphousness came to the fore; and animal forms were able to fulfil important functions here. Perhaps a key work is Giacometti's 'Dog' of 1951 in the Museum of Modern Art, New York. 'It's me,' the artist said of this frayed animal figure, 'one day I saw myself in the street just like that. I was a dog.' Three years later Giacometti produced his 'Cat' in a similar way. Both works recall Kafka's story, 'The Metamorphosis', in which the author describes himself as transformed into an insect.

Theodore Roszak used animal figures in his dramatic sculpture in order to present a fantastic and frightening vision. Again and again his works revolve around the greatest example of American writing, 'Moby Dick'. 'Young Fury' (1950, Pl. 74) and 'Thistle in the Dream' (1955–6) are typical of Roszak's work. The Swiss sculptor Robert Müller also represents animals repeatedly: birds, sea animals, larvae, as well as couplings, organic processes and metamorphoses. A masterwork of nineteenth-century Swiss literature, Jeremias Gotthelf's animal story 'The Black Spider', is plastically expressed in Müller's menacing works.

68 P.A. von Verschaffelt *Group of Deer in Schloßpark Schwetzingen* 18th C.

In England in the '50s animal forms found a rich dissemination. The dramatically agitated figures, combining partly animal and partly human forms, frequently express a defeat. In various works, such as 'Beast XII' of 1957 (Pl. 72), Lynn Chadwick repeatedly uses animal figures—horses, dogs, cattle, birds—as symbols for emotional intensification. Kenneth Armitage attempted to represent the fallen animal in his sculpture ('Roly-Poly' of 1955, Pl. 73). Even his human figures in that period resemble those of animals. As in the work of Chadwick and Germaine Richier, these are hybrids, which express in a typical manner the metamorphosis of the period. Even Eduardo Paolozzi, who was already strongly inclined towards the technical, made use of the animal theme ('Fish' and 'Paris Bird' of 1948).

72 Lynn Chadwick *Beast XII* 1957

73 Kenneth Armitage *Roly-Poly* 1955

71 Constantin Brancusi *Penguins* 1914

75 César *Insecte* 1956

77 David von Schlegell *Untitled* 1965

In France, César ('Scorpion' 1955, 'Insect' 1956, Pl. 75, 'Animal' 1956, 'Fish' 1957) and Germaine Richier created mysterious animal creatures in demonic metamorphoses. Richier's 'Le Griffu' of 1952 (Pl. 3), 'Bull Fight' of 1953, 'Batman' of 1946–56, or 'Horse with Six Heads', show the identification of man and beast, i.e., the animal as a demonic being outfitted with superhuman powers. The Spanish sculptor, Pablo Serrano, concentrated on bulls in his animal sculptures (Pl. 79). In South America, Antonio Berni ('Threatening Bird' of 1965) and Eduardo Jiminez ('Cock in Action') produced fascinating animal images. In the work of Marino Marini, the animal in endless variations has become downright obsessive and turned into a force that cripples the sculptural art. Marini's riders are meant to be embodiments of the earthy and animalistic, expressed through the forms of animals, often in connection with the rider. Most of these works, however, do not rise above an illustrative gesture.

76 Pino Pascali *Ricostruzione del dinosauro* 1966

In the United States, Alexander Calder repeatedly used the animal theme, which is particularly suited to his mobiles and stabiles. Examples are his numerous productions of horses, geese, birds and fish. These have occupied him again and again since his early work in 1930, and reflect his enthusiasm for circuses, indeed for animals themselves. Of his later work, 'The Dog' of 1958 and 'Black Beast' are worth mention; full of joyful fantasy, these are works in which the artist unites ancient animal symbols with the technical laws of our industrial age. Other Americans, such as John Flannagan, Tom Hardy and Anne Arnold, have also produced many animal pieces. In 'Jonah and the Whale' (1937) Flannagan represented the man inside the animal. Hardy's 'Flying Horse' (1957) is a typical example of the 1950s style to which British sculptors have given the most decisive stamp. Anne Arnold, in her woodsculptures—'Elephant' (1963), 'Humpty' (1964), 'Rhinoceros' (1964) and 'Cheetah' (1965)—turned to animal forms of a primitive nature, which seek to bring home the naiveté of animal life. This same effect was apparent in Alexander Iolas' exhibition in 1967 of a zoo by Niki de St Phalle.

78 Charles Frazier *Cow* 1965

79 Pablo Serrano *Taurobolo* 1960

80 Robert Rauschenberg *Monogram* 1959

81 Joseph Cornell *Chocolat Menier* 1952

Thus animal sculpture plays a central role in most recent sculpture; it forms an aspect of the themes sculptors have constantly dealt with right up to the present. Joseph Cornell and Robert Rauschenberg made a new start, using stuffed animals for the effect of authenticity. Cornell's 'Chocolat Menier' (1952, Pl. 81) and Rauschenberg's 'Satellite' (1955), 'Odalisk' (1955–8) and 'Monogram' (1955–9) were pioneer works (Pls. 80 and 83).

82 F. X. Lalanne *Le rhinocéros* 1966

83 Robert Rauschenberg *Odalisk* 1955

Claude and François-Xavier Lalanne made furniture in the likeness of animals, often in herds ('The Rhinoceros' 1966, Pl. 82, and 'Sheep' 1966, Pl. 85), which, through a naturalistic imitation combined with the character of usefulness, enthrone the animal image. In 1967 Mario Ceroli exhibited 'Butterflies' (Pl. 84), and had himself photographed dressed as a butterfly (Pl. 352).

Pino Pascali arrives at an interest in animals from quite different premises: he 'decapitates' giraffes and rhinoceroses (Pl. 87), and represents dolphins, dinosaurs, reptiles and hunters' trophies (Pl. 86). Here the animal stirs the imagination mainly in terms of a subconscious memory.

This is true also of several American sculptors. Like Pascali, David von Schlegell uses elements of non-representative art for his leaping fish and whales (Pl. 77). Charles Frazier's 'Cow' is a surrealistic combination of details of various creatures with monument-like accentuation (Pl. 78). Nicholas Munro goes to the extreme in apparently naturalistic imitation of animals. His work 'Reindeer' (1965) is a manifestation of the animal form as we can see it in a television show, but not in reality. This is concerned with the image, the animal, as it exists today in man's consciousness.

Right:
84 Mario Ceroli *Butterflies* 1967
85 F. X. Lalanne *Les moutons* 1966

86 Pino Pascali *Trofei di caccia* 1966

The result here, too, is the effort to comprise reality unchanged, untransposed, as actual and authentic as possible, in the work of art. Cornell and Rauschenberg were forerunners, and used stuffed, not living, animals. Edward Kienholz, however, used living canaries in his 'tableaux' ('The Wait' of 1964–5) or goldfish ('The State Hospital' of 1964–6). The two reclining male nudes have glass bowls with living goldfish in place of their heads. At an exhibition in Rome, Richard Serra showed a live pig, poultry and other animals. This is clearly a return to baroque universality: in the curio-cabinets of the sixteenth and seventeenth centuries there were not only works of art and curiosities, but also live exotic and native animals. Everything together formed the cosmos of things and creatures which interested man. Are we approaching a period that is also capable of a great cosmic vision?

87 Pino Pascali *La decapitazione delle giraffe*
1966

STILL-LIFE

Except for the work of the ingenious French artist, Bernard Palissy, in the sixteenth century, still-life has played hardly any part in sculpture. This has changed in the immediate present, and still-life has become a dominating subject in the plastic arts. Forerunners of the present trend were the futurists, Dada-ists and surrealists, who early on recognized and revived the ritual character of objects. Giorgio de Chirico drew the whole city as an outdoor still-life. And Umberto Boccioni expressed this new concept in his 'Fusion of a Head and a Window' of 1911. Picasso's plastic still-lifes of 1914 (Pl. 89) were exemplary indications of a newly-won freedom and broke the ground for a new development in this type of sculpture, which culminated in the work of Schwitters. Finally Marcel Duchamp liberated himself from the conventional artistic concepts in his 'ready-mades', creating art from details of reality ('Why Not Sneeze?' of 1921). Man Ray's 'By Itself I' (1918) and Meret Oppenheim's 'Fur-covered Cup, Saucer and Spoon' (1936) evoked associations of subconscious emotional attitudes from objects of everyday use in irrational combinations of meaning.

Today, artists have turned even more intensively towards still-life. Early works of Jasper Johns, such as 'Light Bulb' (1960, Pl. 88) or the food cans cast in bronze and painted (c. 1960), are examples, as well as Robert Morris' human brain pasted over with dollar notes and set in a glass case (Pl. 90). Piero Manzoni's packages and food cans, done between 1959 and 1961, are witnesses of the same obsession and are even more radical than the American compositions. The Czech writer, Jiří Kolář, covers fruit, implements and tools of all sorts with constellations of letters and pictures, and sees in this an extension of his literary possibilities (Pl. 91). This is also an attempt to prove that there are no frontiers. What Kolář would like above all is to cover the Prague Opera House entirely with his writings. This idea is not unlike Christo's desire to wrap a whole building in plastic material and string (Pl. 278).

88 Jasper Johns *Light Bulb* 1960

64

89 Pablo Picasso *Still-Life* 1914

90 Robert Morris *Untitled* 1963–1964

91 Jiří Kolář *Appleand Pear* 1964

Literature plays a part in the still-lifes of Gianfranco Baruchello ('Partout le silence sans mouvement' of 1962) and H. C. Westermann. In his work 'Westermann's Table' (1966), the artist built up a pyramid of books in the style of a monument (Pl. 92). On the whole, the book has taken on an archetypal significance in modern sculpture. In John Latham's work it is the central theme, particularly in a destroyed form. The books are all burned and then made into the subject and material of the work. In Lucas Samaras' 'Book No. 6' (1962), the book has taken on the character of a fetish. Paul van Hoeydonck has used books as symbols in his cosmic environments (Pl. 93). Similarly, the Swede, Erik Dietmann, has wrapped books in adhesive tape, i.e., packed them up and defunctionalized them. Like Kolář, Kusama and Christo, Dietmann has obsessively extended this principle to all things—to pieces of clothing, furniture, books and much more. For his 'Poet' of 1960, George Herms set bundled manuscripts on a wooden base, thus attempting to create his effect through real objects and no longer through metaphor.

The doll as a symbol of the subconscious—as already in surrealism—plays a role in the works of Joseph Cornell (Pl. 95), Yayoi Kusama (Pl. 361), Bernhard Höke (Pl. 96) and Paul van Hoeydonck (Pl. 97), and also to a great extent in Happenings.

A traditional category of this art species, the world of cookery and the subject-matter of food, has also been widely applied in new works of still-life. Man Ray already used this subject in his 'Mr Knife and Mrs Fork' of 1944. Prefabricated industrial products, e.g., Coca Cola bottles, have also been incorporated in plastic compositions by Robert Rauschenberg ('Coca Cola Plan' of 1958) and Westermann ('White for Purity', 1959–60). Trova, Kusama, Ay-O, Lichtenstein, Watts and Roy Adzak have represented dining

92 H. C. Westermann *Westermann's Table* 1966

93 Paul van Hoeydonck *The Unwritten Spacebooks* 1965

Right:
94 Jim Dine *Black Hand Saw* 1962

tables or table-settings. Tom Wesselmann has particularly devoted himself to this field in his pictures, which have consistently been aiming towards plastic qualities. In 'Still-Life' of 1964 he portrayed a bottle, an orange and a radio-set—not painted, but the real things attached to a wall-board (Pl. 98).

The most important artist in this genre is Claes Oldenburg, whose 'Viandes', 'Hamburgers' and 'Patisseries' are witnesses of an aggressive and propelling obsession (Pls. 105 and 106). Lucy R. Lippard has said of them: 'They are appealing because they combine gaiety with elephantine sadness.' Oldenburg himself said: 'This is not art, it's a hamburger!' but also made this unequivocal statement: 'If I didn't think what I was doing had something to do with enlarging the boundaries of art, I wouldn't go on doing it.'

The vinyl compositions Oldenburg has made in the last few years out of soft plastics —the first of these was 'Soft Typewriter' (1963)—show that this artist recognizes no boundaries and works to transform the consumers' world that surrounds us. His ensemble 'Falling Shoestring Potatoes' of 1965, which presents exactly what its title suggests, transcends, so to speak, the species still-life and is in fact a contradictio in adjecto. This is in no way diminished by the power of the artistic effect. Most recently Oldenburg has made sketches for gigantic monuments of teddy-bears, hot-dogs and ironing-boards.

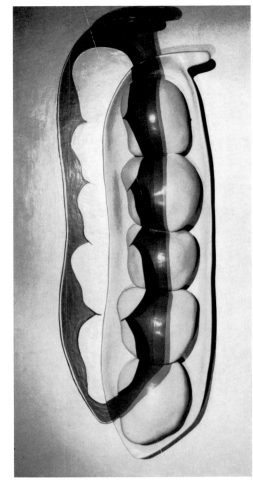

99 Marjorie Strider *Double Bean* 1965

98 Tom Wesselmann *Still-Life* 1964

Right:
100 Michael Sandle *Orange and Lemons* 1966

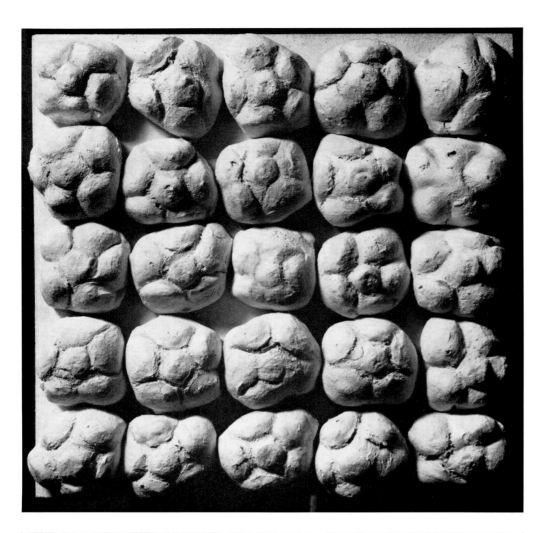

102 Piero Gilardi *Cabbages under the Snow*
1966

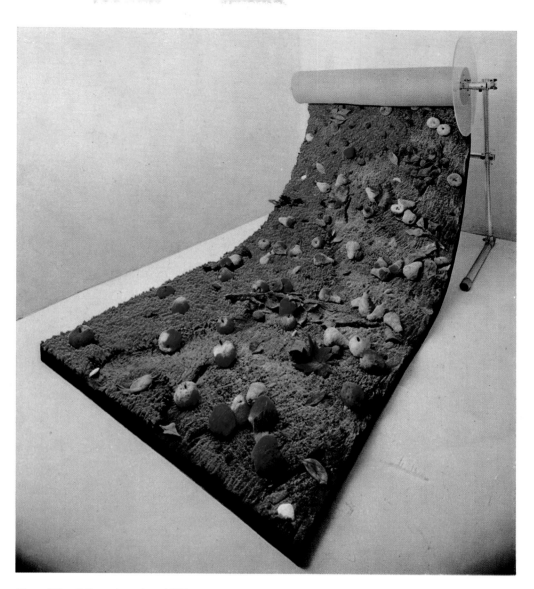

Piero Gilardi *Tappeto natura* 1967

103 Paul Thek *Untitled* 1966

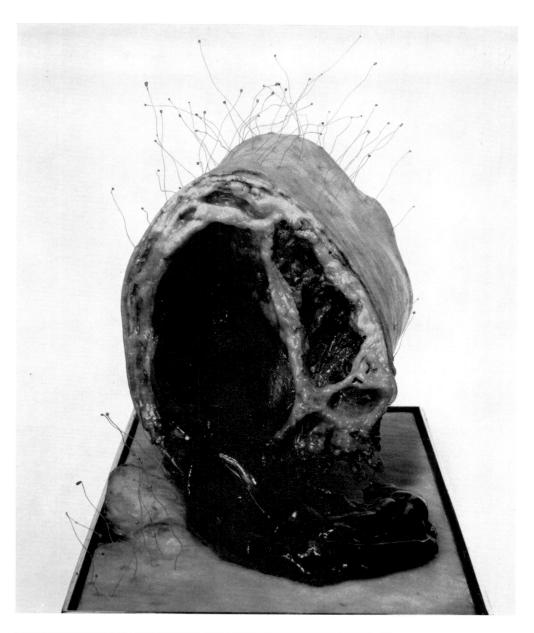

104 Peter Agostini *Egg Pile* 1964

105 Claes Oldenburg *Viandes* 1964

106 Claes Oldenburg *Pâtisserie* 1964

Right:
107 Otto Mühl *Materialaktion Stilleben* 1964
108 Otto Mühl *Materialaktion Stilleben* 1964

74

109 Martial Raysse *Tricolore Modern Painting* 1964
110 Michelangelo Pistoletto *Pistoletto's New Work* 1965

Artists such as Piero Manzoni (Pl. 101), Piero Gilardi (Pl. 102), Paul Thek (Pl. 103), Marjorie Strider, Peter Agostini (Pl. 104), Michael Sandle (Pl. 100), Wayne Thibaud and Robert Watts have also handled this same theme. Thek copied a large joint of meat covered with mould (Pl. 103). He is preoccupied with decomposition, transformation, the transition of one material into another. Marjorie Strider conceived of a bean-pod ('Double Bean' of 1965) with unusual dimensions (Pl. 99). Wayne Thibaud created huge painted sweets ('Candy Cane' of 1965) and Robert Watts 'Hot Dogs' (1964), 'Rye-Bread Study' (1964) and 'Bacon, Lettuce and Tomato' (1965), Michael Sandle 'Orange and Lemons' (Pl. 100). Daniel Spoerri added real foods and cooking implements to his programmatic presentations of breakfast trays ('Kiki's Breakfast' of 1960), and revealed new possibilities in this category. Spoerri also gives cooking demonstrations, thus bringing his plastic fixation into action.

In this category, too, the result lies in the action of materials, as can be seen, for example, in Otto Mühl's compositions in Vienna. In a Happening 'Still-life' in 1964

111 Gino Marotta *Fiore* 1967

(Pls. 107 and 108), Otto Mühl confronted people with objects, and both the animate and inanimate were used as elements of a creation directed towards new objectives. It is not fortuitous that food and cuisine play a leading role in Happenings.

In extending the facilities of painting, Jim Dine has incorporated real tools into his pictures ('Black Hand Saw' of 1962, Pl. 94). Niki de St Phalle also favoured hand tools in an earlier phase of her development ('Tu est moi' of 1960). Arman's screw-propellors arranged on a flat surface stand midway between his 'accumulations' and the laws of op art inherited from other traditions (Pl. 161). Jean Pierre Raynaud gives the name 'Psycho-objects' to his works built up out of walls, parts of walls, tubes, receptacles and instruments; in combination, the things he uses take on a new meaning (Pl. 159).

A special form of this category is flower still-life, of which there are numerous examples today. Martial Raysse's 'Tricolore Modern Painting' (1964) is a potted plant made out of neon-tubes (Pl. 109). The Dutch artist Ferdi makes flowers of dangerous beauty out of plastic. In 1967 in Rome, the Greek Jannis Kounellis exhibited flowers which shot a flame out of their centres (Pls. 304 and 305). Michelangelo Pistoletto (Pl. 110), Marjorie Strider (Pl. 112), Gino Marotta (Pls. 111 and 365), Mario Ceroli and many others have been concerned with flowers. New conceptions of an approach to reality with the use of fruit or flower still-lifes have been developed by Alik Cavaliere and Billy Apple, who has adopted the name of his main subject. Apple's still-life '2 Minutes, 3.3 Seconds' of 1962 shows three apples at different stages of consumption.

112 Marjorie Strider *Double Flower* 1965

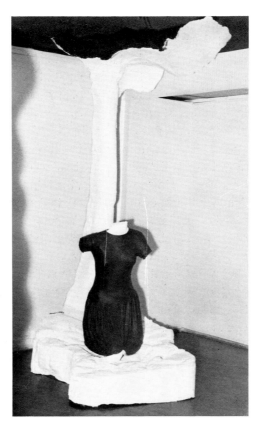

113 Yayoi Kusama *Flower Coat* 1963

114 Ivor Abrahams *Red Riding Hood* 1963

CLOTHING

Clothing is another of the elements that play a special role in the work of today's artists. It is not only that they design clothing or cloth; they also incorporate articles of clothing into their compositions, or use them as the materials of their art. Artists like Oldenburg and Dine ('Angels for Lorca' of 1966, Pl. 116) have made clothing a central theme; frequently they have painted clothing or produced it out of coloured plastic. Oldenburg's 'Giant Blue Pants' of 1962 was quite unjustifiably misunderstood; the artist was not in any sense using a bought object, but creating the trousers anew (like his typewriter, his hamburger and his furniture) and turning them into a work of art.

Paul Harris has built whole rooms out of cloth and animated them with figures in expensive clothes. Parts of clothing are the centre and theme of Ivor Abrahams' large cast-pieces ('Red Riding Hood', 1963, Pl. 114).

In the work of Kusama, Christo, Eielson and Berlant, cloth and articles of clothing are used in such a way that the element of wear remains a component of the total effect. Yayoi Kusama's dresses and shoes (Pl. 113), the shirts of Christo, Eielson and Berlant, contain traces of wear even when they are changed, raised out of the real consumers' world and transformed with imaginative freedom. The use of clothing in Happenings is also deliberate. To choose one example: as early as 1957 Atsuko Tanaka presented 'Fantastic Garments for the Stage' in the Happenings of the Japanese group, Gutai (Pl. 115). Her garments, in part decorated with many small and large light bulbs, transcended the commonplace object and formed a particularly fascinating contribution to the Japanese demonstrations.

115 Atsuko Tanaka *Fantastic Garments for the Stage* 1957

FURNITURE

The most intimate thing in man's environment is the room in which he lives and amuses himself, works or sleeps—and its furnishings. Hence this subject especially engages the new artists; indeed many of them, as in the case of clothing, directly influence the design of these things. The artist's desire to use his art on things of daily use is not a new one. It has determined the development of art for a longer time than the sharp distinction by which the artist was restricted to art and the craftsman to objects of utility. In early times, even in the Middle Ages, such limitations were not recognized in almost all civilizations. And today artists occupy themselves once again with objects of utility.

The art nouveau artists (Gaudí, Pl. 122, Mackintosh, Loos) were already concerned with man's environment in the widest sense (furniture, implements, clothing, gardens). Aside from the important works of twentieth-century architects and furniture-designers (Mies van der Rohe, Marcel Breuer, Mart Stam, Gerrit Thomas Rietveld, Alvar Aalto, Charles Eames, Eero Saarinen), all of whom had artistic characteristics typical of their period, artists of today like Isamu Noguchi (tables, benches), Arman (spiral armchair), Philotas (garden chair), Day Schnabel (table),

117 Robert Watts *Chair* 1966

118 Joseph Beuys *Stuhl mit Fett* 1963

James Guitet (cupboards), Philippe Hiquily (tables), Günter Uecker (bed) and many others are concerned with the design of furniture. The futurist painter Balla designed a bedroom already before the First World War. Following that, the piece of furniture was transformed and given emotional qualities. Victor Brauner's 'Wolf Table' (1939) and Kurt Seligmann's 'Ultrameuble' (1938) are early examples of this. Rauschenberg, Kusama, Samaras, Pistoletto, Höke (Pl. 124) and Uecker have used the bed as theme. In his 'Bedroom' of 1963, Oldenburg extended this into an environment which, with its proportions distorted in the style of furniture catalogues, became an alarming vision. In his cupboard-piece 'About a Black Magic Maker' (1959–60), Westermann tried to achieve something similar through a craftsmanlike perfection of apparent absurdity. Chairs and sofas appear repeatedly, and with their accompanying images, dreams, wishes, longings and anxieties. Kusama covers armchairs, sofas, chests, tables and chairs with phallic forms or coloured nets (Pl. 120). Dietmann may paste up a cast-off three-legged table with adhesive tape. Uecker hammers nails into stools, tables (Pl. 120) and pianos. The objects look as if attacked, they begin to proliferate, they take on an aggressive meaningfulness through their programmatic defunction-alization. Stefan Wewerka broke chairs in half and produced a new unreal spatial

119 Lucas Samaras *Untitled* 1965

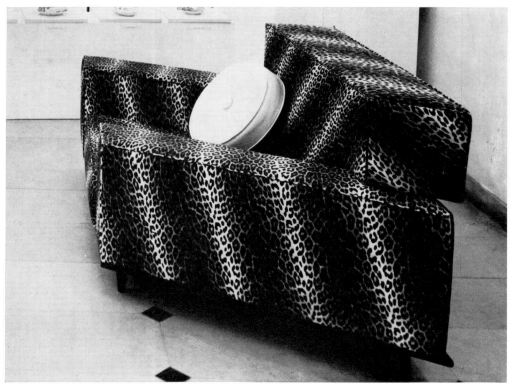

121 Claes Oldenburg *Armchair* 1964

122 Antoni Gaudí *Specchiera*

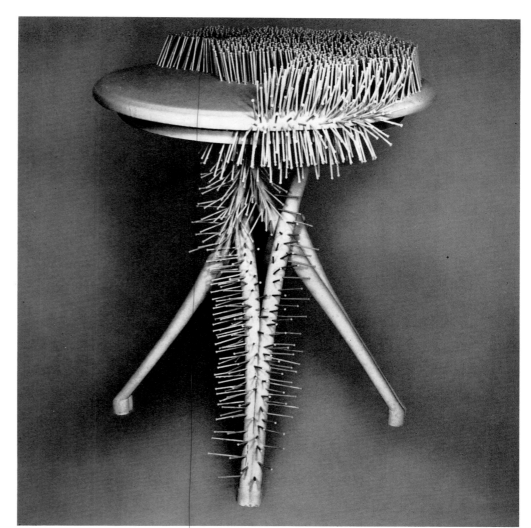

123 Günter Uecker *Transgression* 1962

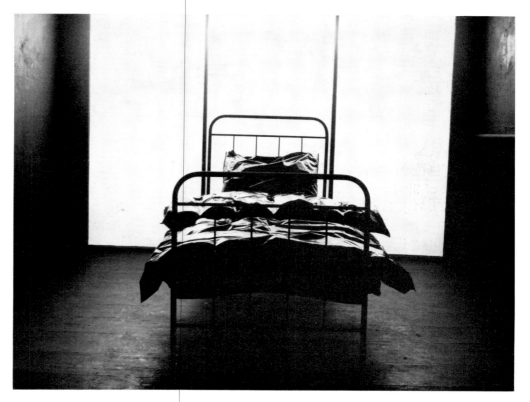

124 Bernhard Höke *Folien-Bett* 1965

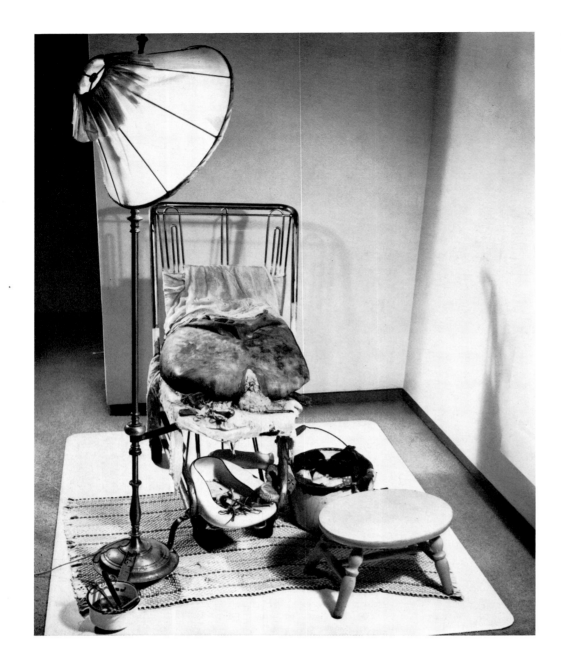

situation out of the two parts. Robert Watts outlined the contours of his chair with light-tubes (Pl. 117). In the work of Kienholz and Kudo, deck-chairs are symbols of man's basic experiences, mute witnesses, left-over objects which bear the traces of use and the users (Pls. 125 and 126). In his tableaux, Kienholz has gone over to a demonic transformation of entire rooms with all their furnishings (Pls. 127 and 128).

In contrast, Richard Artschwager uses table and chair not as the real objects of our environment, but in the sense of conscious symbol-structures. His untitled work with table and chair (1963) and his 'Table with Table-cloth' (1964) are works in the style of primary structures. They obliterate the objective relationship. The Japanese, Jiro Takamatsu, exhibited in 1967 in the Matsuya Department Store in Tokyo his illusionist relief-construction 'Desk and Four Chairs'. As in Oldenburg's bedroom, the intention here is the inducement of distortion. Lucas Samaras has constructed similar basic

models of table and chair entirely out of mirrors and placed them in a room of mirrors. Through endless superimpositions of contours, through light and reflection, they lose any outline—all distinctions between appearance and reality are cancelled. Other furniture pieces by Lucas Samaras, like the 'Chairs' (1965) overgrown with wool and needles, are again expressions of an obsession (Pl. 119). Their overgrown forms articulate primitive experiences, press into the region of instinct, seem to expose secret vices and forbidden desires as if by means of a residue of magic. It is not accidental that this type of presentation has been related to the effects of LSD.

In his work 'Green Table and Chairs', shown in 1966 at the Sidney Janis Gallery in an exhibition of erotic art, Jim Dine coordinated his furniture pieces in a manner calculated to produce erotic associations. Through manifold relations of meaning, subliminal images were brought to light, without one's being able to identify them or to explain

721 Edward Kienholz *While Visions of Sugar Plums Danced in Their Heads* 1965

the work of art unequivocally. Joseph Beuys filled the space between the back and seat of an old kitchen chair with plastic material (Pl. 118). A space created for a particular purpose and adapted to that purpose, is made unusable for exactly that purpose.

Pre-existing and added things merge at a new level to create together, without formal means, a new area of meaning whose message can no longer be discovered rationally. In the great works of earlier art, too, the meaning is always ambiguous, no matter how strong the inclination to assume otherwise. Because of our familiarity with the forms of the past this is not immediately evident; but in the new art it cannot be evaded. Art possesses truths which go beyond understanding and communication, indeed art begins exactly where unequivocal understanding leaves off.

128 Edward Kienholz *While Visions of Sugar
Plums Danced in Their Heads* (part.) 1965

MODERN MEANS OF TRANSPORTATION

Modern man is dependent on means of locomotion to a degree formerly unknown. Therefore the images of aeroplanes, automobiles, motorcycles and ships play a particular role in the subject-matter of contemporary art. Especially the automobile appears repeatedly not only in painting (Copley, Wesselmann, Rosenquist, Hamilton, etc.) but also in sculpture. It contains a multiplicity of meanings. It is not just a status symbol, a measure of social respectability, but it is also associated with erotic visions, on the one hand as a means of enhancing its owner's attractiveness, and on the other as a scene of erotic relations. At the same time, this image encompasses the moment of danger, the imagining of disaster, murder, blood and death. Its most lapidary expression is the identification of man and automobile in General Motors' advertising slogan: 'Life is just one Cadillac after another'.

Among outstanding examples of the use of automobiles in sculpture are Marisol's 'Four People in a Car' (1964), Edward Kienholz's 'Back Seat Dodge' (1964, Pl. 129 and IV), Charles Frazier's 'Drag Racer' (1966, Pl. 130), Salvatore Scarpitta's 'Rajo Jack Special'' (1964, Pl. 131) and Ernest Trova's 'Carman' (1966). In the work of other artists, it is the distorted form of the automobile which serves as the material for sculpture.

Edward Kienholz *Back Seat Dodge – '38* 1964

132 Pino Pascali *Barca* 1965

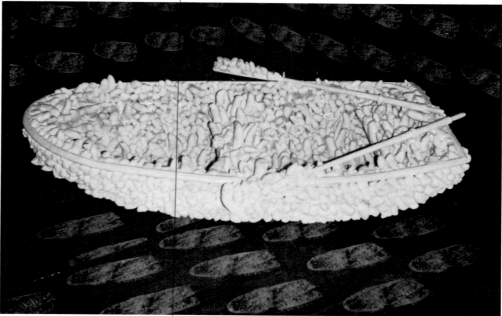

133 Yayoi Kusama *One Thousand Boat Show*
1965

Chamberlain, Seley and César use it in this way. Robert Rauschenberg has used parts, such as doors, in large constructions. The automobile also plays a distinctive role in Happenings. In 1960, Jim Dine arranged his Happening 'The Car Crash'; in the Swedish Happening of 1964, 'Tributes and Floor Plans', Rose-Marie Larsson was married to a mini-car.

Among fascinating representations of the ship, Kusama's 'One Thousand Boat Show' (Pl. 133) and Pascali's 'Barca' (Pl. 132) should be mentioned.

LANDSCAPE

In the previous development of art, landscape was essentially a subject for painting; sculptors, using quite different media, ventured into this field only rarely. Ghiberti's Doors of Paradise on the Baptistery in Florence could certainly vie with the works of contemporary paintings, even though the colour effects were restricted to shining surfaces of bronze and other metals. Landscape plays a similar role in Rodin's work, in which it may be said to take in a larger scope.

The most recent sculpture, stretching beyond all boundaries for its thematic materials, has not stopped at landscape either. Henry Moore's figures have been interpreted as landscapes (Pl. 1). Peter Agostini called one of his pieces 'Woman Landscape'. Emil Cimiotti ('Suspended Landscape', 1962) and Brigitte Meier-Denninghoff have also tried to represent landscape in sculpture. The plastic landscapes of the new art differ from those attempts in the style of presentation as well as in their materials. The works in painting and sculpture of Tom Wesselmann, Roy Lichtenstein, Allan d'Arcangelo and Pino Pascali (Pl. 137) originate essentially from this theme. In 'View from a Window' (1965, Pl. 134), Marjorie Strider created plastically a landscape of clouds out of large suspended forms. Also Warhol's floating silver cushions (Pl. 294), Haacke's air-plastics (Pl. 295) and Christo's wrapped balloons can be interpreted as landscapes (Pls. 297 and 298).

New aspects are offered by the various attempts to attain ever greater authenticity, to incorporate topographical fragments as realistically as possible into artistic constructions. The Italian, Piero Gilardi, uses plastic to create deceptive imitations of soil, stones, vegetable beds (Pl. 102 and III).

The seascape is also a popular subject again. Gilardi's 'Mouettes sur la mer' is a 'seascape' with whitecaps and gulls. Gilardi says, 'I have faith in our technological civilization, for it can reproduce the facts of nature, triumphing over death.' In 'Il Mare', Pino Pascali made an image of environmental art with the means of optical-constructive art (Pl. 338). The dolphins, projecting out of the wall above the 'sea', extend the real, accidental space and at the same time attest to the aim of ironic alienation. In 'Bagged Seascape with Green Cruiser' (1966), Jain Baxter also treated the seascape ironically.

134 Marjorie Strider *View From a Window* 1965

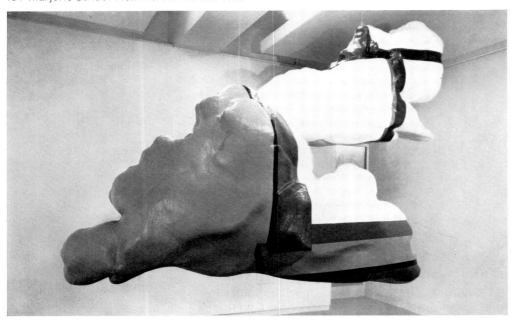

135 Gino Marotta *Albero* 1967

Lucio Fontana's new reliefs since 1965 are also representations of landscape. In his sculpture, the American, Robert Graham, uses landscape, in the style of knick-knackcopies, as the backdrop of the erotic. His most recent constructions in plexi-glass cases, based solely on the colour-spatial effect of blue sky and white clouds, are masterpieces of a new landscape sculpture (Pl. 136). In 'The Gates of Times Square' (Pl. 322), Chryssa used the landscape of the world-city's centre as the theme of her neon sculpture.

Primitive visions of Paradise in the representation of gardens, as evident especially towards the end of the Middle Ages and in art nouveau, appear again in the spatial 'accumulations' of Martial Raysse ('Heart Garden', Pl. 329), Yayoi Kusama ('Narcissus Garden', Pl. 342), Anne Truit ('Sea Garden'), Jean Tinguely and Niki de St-Phalle ('Jardin fantastique') and Günter Uecker ('Zero Garden', Pl. 374). The numerous garden exhibitions, in which sculpture is still incorporated, are equally new manifestations of the ancient symbolism (Pl. 281). Pascal's explanation of the fact that a longing deeply anchored in man for the lost Paradise was expressed in gardens, was that man went astray in a garden but was also saved in one.

Sculpture is on the way to rediscovering our environment and disclosing hidden emotional elements in it. Therefore the role of environment in today's art is no accident. We stand at the beginning of an epoch which, like the advances of the waning Middle Ages, explores not only in unfamiliar and distant regions, but also in the unknown and unused areas of our immediate surroundings—in the commonplace, technified and long-despised reality.

In surrealism, transformation and metamorphosis already played a role: a thing was not only what it appeared to be, but at the same time—by being given a name or a double meaning—it became something else. The clarity of objects was suspended; one turned into another; nothing was assured or enduring, but rather transitional, relative, ambiguous, immanent, mysterious and puzzling. Today these phenomena are distinctly moving onto a new plane.

In the new presentation of objects the essential factor is the ready-made, the pre-fixed, the prefabricated. This can be achieved on the one hand with the use of waste-products of our civilization. Lawrence Alloway has interpreted the origins of what he calls 'junk culture' as follows: 'The source of junk culture is obsolescence, the throw-away material of cities, as it collects in drawers, closets, attics, garbage cans, gut-ters, waste lots, and city dumps.' The objects of everyday use have their own history to start with, and then have another specific effect when deprived of their original function. They become relics of human life, and retain this character even when they are incorporated into new contexts that are alien to their essence. Picasso's 'Bull's Head (Pl. 70) of 1942 is an early typical example of this sort of alienation of banal, everyday things, divorced from their original relationships and transplanted into a new complex through the artistic imagination.

138 Joseph Cornell *Postage Stamp Box*
1960–1965

139 Robert Rauschenberg *Aenfloga* 1961

A second possibility for exploiting the ready-made is in the use of new objects of our daily environment: vacuum cleaners, refrigerators, music-boxes and machines. The futurists and Dada-ists already included industrial mass-produced objects among the materials of their art. Umberto Boccioni consistently urged the abandonment of restrictions on the plastic arts to specific materials. He declared that a work could perfectly well consist of twenty different materials, that one could use glass, wood, iron, cement, hair, leather, cloth, even electric light, in the field of art.

Forerunners in this use of the reality that surrounds us are Marcel Duchamp, Kurt Schwitters, the surrealists and Joseph Cornell (Pls. 81, 95 and 138). The latter's boxes contain objects ranged together which are taken out of other contexts and obtain a new complexity of effectiveness in their new juxtaposition—which has a documentary character and yet cannot be analyzed. Alexandra Cortesi has said: 'The box presents a microcosm, in which the objects communicate primarily among themselves; a kind of "sacred conversation", which records an aspect of certain kinds of still-life, goes on among the objects within the box.'

In Europe the related artistic movement of Nouveau Réalisme is concentrated in Paris. Tinguely (Pls. 142–144) and César (Pls. 6 and 149) use the waste-products of big-city civilization. After his mobile sculpture of the 1950s, his so-called 'metaméchaniques', Jean Tinguely progressed in the 60s to compositions of a Happening type; the most famous of these was the 'Machine-happening auto-destructive' which

140 Robert Mallary *Little Hans* 1962

141 Yayoi Kusama *Handbag* 1965

he showed at the Museum of Modern Art, New York, on 17 March 1960 as a 'Homage to New York'. It was simultaneously a work and a demonstration. Sculptures like 'Peak Production' and 'Samurai' (1963, Pl. 142) create a combination, without any apparent meaning, out of wheels, transmission-belts and guillotine-like metal parts, which has menacing as well as ironic characteristics. 'Nicator' of 1966 (Pls. 143 and 144) is a composition of this type at its most extreme and most simplified. In 1966 'Heureka' was publicly exhibited in Zürich: an emotion machine, in which mechanized man could recognize himself as a thinking machine. Like Tinguely, Abraham Palatnik assembles mobile constructions out of metal parts, wheels and belts; in form, colour and sound these demonstrate a harmony of pointless theatre. The fluid transference from construction to action is as evident in this type of work as in all categories of contemporary sculpture.

César pressed metal scraps of chassis and motors, found in automobile graveyards, into heavy blocks, which he treated as symbols of a new realism. He was seeking a quite different sort of realism, however, in the red polystyrene thumb he produced in 1965: 'Le Pouce de César' shows again the artist's striving for the greatest possible authenticity (Pl. 57). Like Tinguely and César (Pl. 149), the Italian Ettore Colla (Pl. 145), the Dane Robert Jacobsen, the Japanese Tajiri, the American Mark di Suvero (Pl. 146) and the Frenchman Viseux have used parts of old metal in their works, remains of implements and machines, found pieces robbed of their function. Richard Stankiewicz consistently uses waste-products for his sculptures, and has created out of them suggestive forms of an anti-functional meaning which is reminiscent of Tinguely's work. Fairfield Porter wrote of Stankiewicz: 'His sculpture, using junk, is a creation of life out of death, the new life being of a quite different nature than the old one that was decaying on the junk pile, on the sidewalks, in the used car lot.' The Yugoslav Dusan Dzamonya uses nothing but rusty nails in his works, which most closely approximate the fetish character of primitive art.

In the United States, along with Stankiewicz—after a new evaluation of the work of Joseph Cornell and Kurt Schwitters—Robert Rauschenberg, Jasper Johns, Robert Morris and John Chamberlain also contributed to a specifically American expression of these objectives. Johns and Rauschenberg proceeded from painting, first to relief and ultimately to sculpture. For instance, in his 'Monogram' (1955–9, Pl. 80), Rauschenberg coordinated a stuffed goat and an automobile tyre on a painted surface. In his 'Odalisk' (1955–8), he starts with a foot resting on a cushion; on the foot is a box, treated in the style of his painting with photographs and colours; the box is crowned by a stuffed rooster (Pl. 83). Jasper Johns was inclined, perhaps even earlier than Rauschenberg, to exploit the prefabricated consumers' world of everyday America (Pl. 88). He not only reproduced food-cans, articles of clothing and implements, but also made use of specific emotional clichés which determine the attitudes of the average American. Johns and Rauschenberg (who has finally gone over to Happenings as Tinguely has done) nevertheless remain essentially painters.

142 Jean Tinguely *Samurai* 1963

143 Jean Tinguely *Nicator* 1966

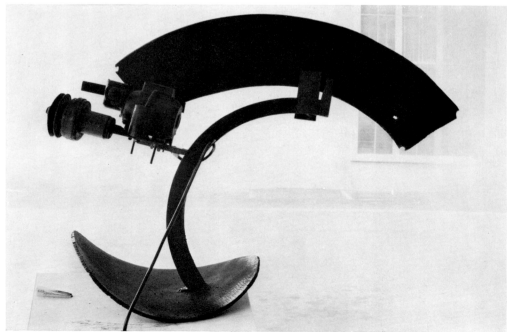

144 Jean Tinguely *Nicator* 1966

Right:
146 Mark di Suvero *New York Dawn* 1965

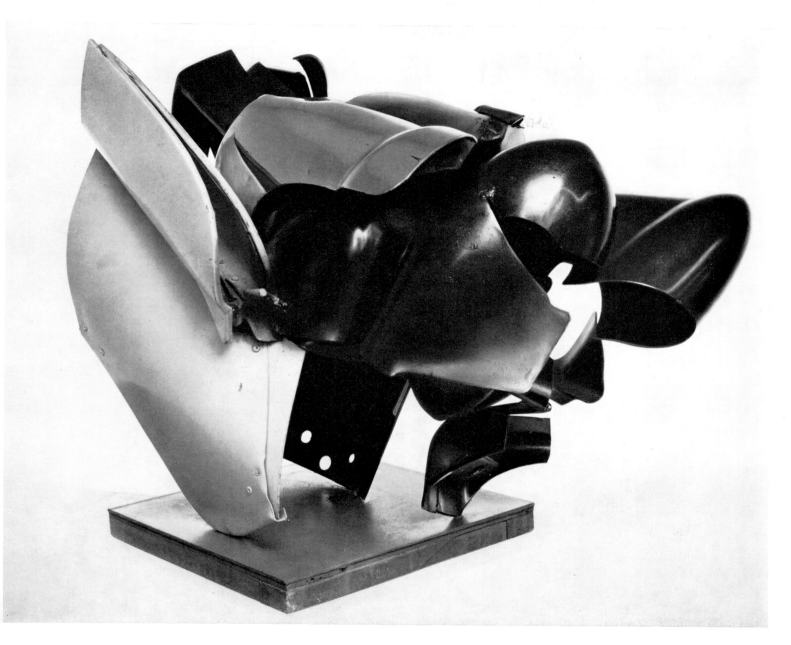

148 John Chamberlain *Slauson* 1964

John Chamberlain (Pls. 147 and 148) and Jason Seley (Pls. 150 and 151) also use automobile chassis for their sculpture as César does in France, but in an entirely different
way. Chamberlain assembles battered components which, merely through their colours, recall their original useful purpose. Seley welds the polished chrome parts of
cars into new configurations. Both artists agree on the dominating ritual role of the
automobile in modern civilization. Their theme is the destroyed object which they present in quite new guises. On the other hand, Charles Frazier, in 'Drag Racer' (1966,
Pl. 130), handles the theme in the traditional surrealist manner. Mark di Suvero pro-
ceeds from still other premises and builds his sculptures out of found wood and metal
parts (Pl. 146). His surprising spatial combinations, such as 'Queen's Rook' (1962–3),
which have a figurative effect, are often stimulated by found, already-used forms. For
example, the arrangement of 'Bach Peace' (1962–3, Scull Collection) is entirely dictated by a railway sleeper. In 'Mother and Child' (1962), too, di Suvero was concerned
with figurative assimilations.

Left:
147 John Chamberlain *Big E* 1962

149 César *Petit panneau* 1958

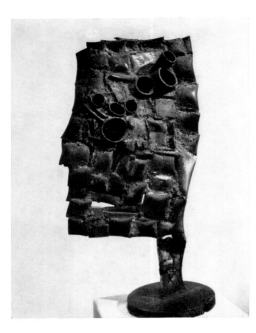

150 Jason Seley *Pas encore* 1965

Robert Mallary makes objects out of wood, polyester, steel, cloths and many other already existing materials; hung or mounted, these give a frightening impression. Mallary subordinates everything to a fantasy magic, which frequently brings to mind the horrors of fairy-tales ('Fallen Angels', 1962; 'Little Hans', 1962, Pl. 140), and is meant to oppress the viewer. Somewhat similar is the idol developed out of a used object (in this case a hanging handbag) by Yayoi Kusama; like Kusama's furniture, implements and environments, this gives expression to a clearly pansexual ritual (Pl. 141).

The American, Lee Bontecou, has also shown a kind of obsession in her works assembled from cloths, metals, railings, canvas and wires (Pls. 152–154). Her objects with holes and bulges, which have a totem-like effect, are as much a symbolic expression of the basic sex-wish as Kusama's objects overgrown with phalluses or nets. Lee Bontecou's large work (all this artist's pieces are untitled) in the New York State Theater at Lincoln Center has a totem character which gives visual expression, in monumental form, to the fantasies of the masses.

Edward Kienholz likewise contrasts and combines found objects, raises them out of their utter meaninglessness and makes something new emerge. In objects like 'Blind Ignus' (Pl. 155) and 'Ella Cry' (Pl. 156), fragments of reality are incorporated in such a way that the meaning of the original real context remains a component of the newly-created cosmos. Related works have been made in Germany by H. P. Alvermann and in Italy by Elio Marchegiani. For his 'Hommage à Helena Rubenstein' (1964), Alvermann attached a hairdrying machine and an animal skull to a board (Pl. 158). Marchegiani attained similar results in early works such as 'Vecchia storia' (1965) and 'Progetto per una lapide luminosa a James Bond' (1965), with that striving for mastery of form which is innate in Europeans (Pl. 157).

Pino Pascali assembles cannons out of automobile tyres, plywood and tubes, which make clear the fetish character of new sculpture, in line with our modern reality. In 1965–6 he created a series called 'Armi' (Pl. 164). The 'Colomba della Pace' of 1965 should not have been misunderstood as a demonstration of pacifism. A bomb 6 meters long was so perfectly imitated and shown in so many various exhibitions that one might well speak of 'frozen Happenings'.

Left:
152 Lee Bontecou *Untitled* 1964
153 Lee Bontecou *Untitled* 1962

154 Lee Bontecou *Untitled* 1964

The young artists of today are no longer concerned with the emphasis of social criticism, with aggression, but rather with a dispassionate statement of things as they are. Therefore an abundance of meanings and contents are offered, combined with one another and alienated in a merry, vicious and ironic manner. Pascali's 'Bomba della Pace' is the bomb as threat as well as guarantee of peace: it exists as both in political clichés. It is the emphasized symbol of mass deployment, the historical showpiece of military museums, the fetish of enemies at war, and at the same time—through the ironic title—it is again none of these things. Finally the rhyme 'Bomba' and 'Colomba' in Italian is also significant.

Another possibility for transcending the things that surround and concern us is taking over unused technical machinery. In this way industrial products are incorporated into works of art, or declared to be works of art. Here, too, Marcel Duchamp was a pioneer in creating new, unsuspected associations of meaning through his challenging titles.

Right:
156 Edward Kienholz *Ella Cry* 1962

In more recent times this has also been the practice, for example, of the Frenchman Sanejouand, who uses synthetics and throws a new light on them by framing them, arranging them in rows, or putting them on pedestals (Pl. 163). Raynaud's 'Psycho-objects', also made in France, were based on the same idea (Pl. 159). In Germany, Bernard Höke and H.P. Alvermann (Pl. 158) used similar methods, and in England, Michael Sandle produced new forms out of technical components which he called e.g. 'Crocus' (1963–4). In the United States, Charles Mattox, John Bennett (Pl. 160) and Philip Makanna, above all, should be mentioned in this connection. Also in the work of George Brecht there are numerous examples of this type, and John Chamberlain went through a similar phase around 1966.

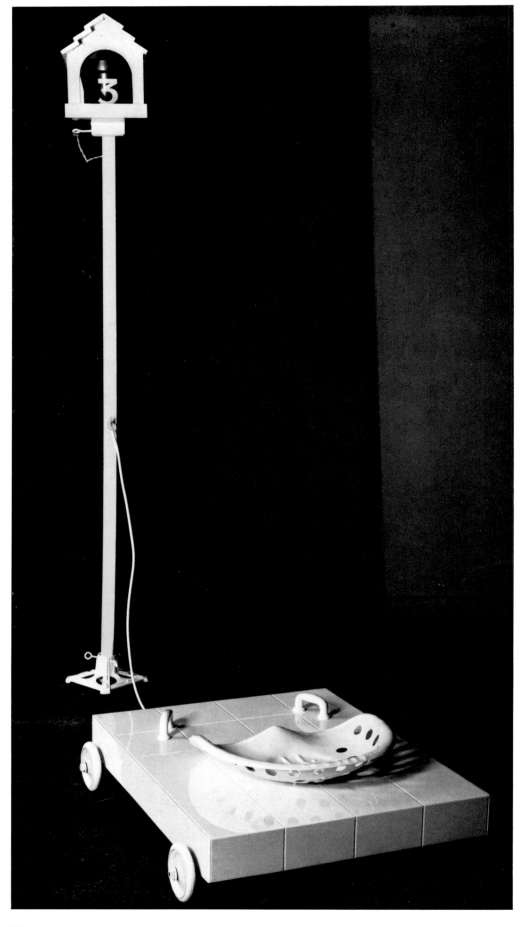

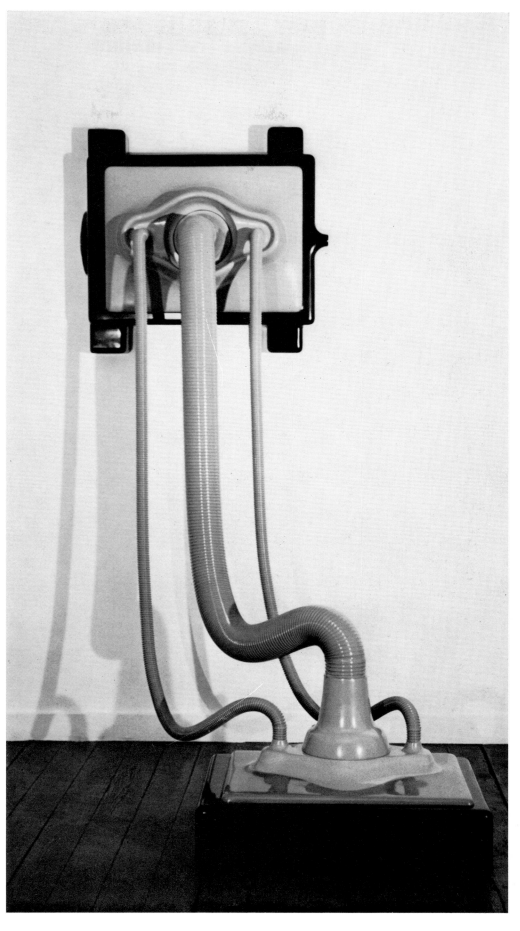

Right:
162 Les Levine *Plug Assist* 1966
163 Sanejouand *81 cubitenairs* 1965

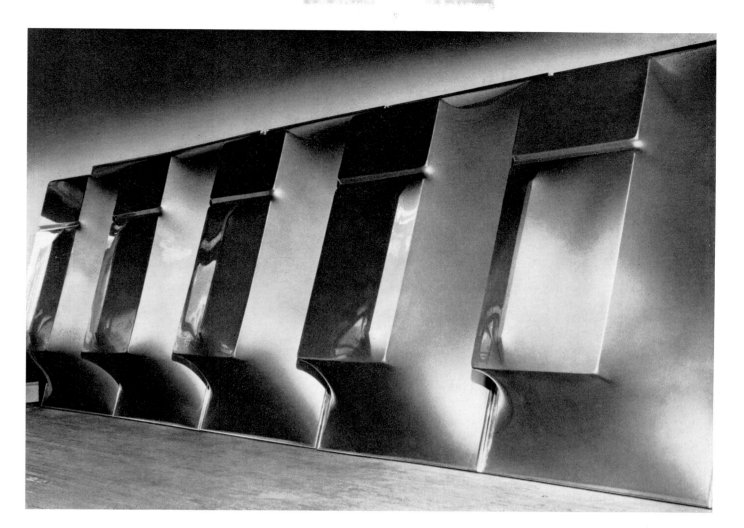

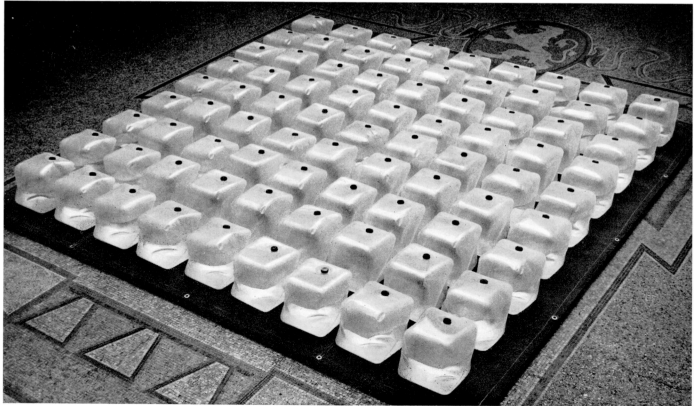

164 Pino Pascali *Armi* 1966

Les Levine transformed useful objects, such as chairs, by casting them; the cast remains as a reminder of the object which no longer exists (Pl. 162). Technical forms, not only of already used or used-up consumers' goods, but also of those that come onto the market brand-new and pristine, have become the material of the artistic fantasy and have unlocked whole new areas.

For most people the creative transposition of real objects into the reality of art is difficult to understand. But in the light of results so far, it cannot be doubted that this is a legitimate form of artistic endeavour. The demand for authenticity, for an ever stronger penetration into reality, is evident everywhere. This effort does not stop at the mass-produced articles of daily consumption. It is important that, following the phase of a language which translated reality with the methods of metaphor, image and comparison, and an effort to master reality with formal methods, we have moved today into a phase of the unchanged, untranslated adoption of our environment into a realism which can harmonize man with his world in a way that befits our epoch.

Gino Marotta *Aleph* 1964

IV NEW WAYS IN SPACE

Richard Stankiewicz has ironically outlined the immeasurable breadth of today's artistic possibilities: 'If current sculpture is classed in oppositions such as figurative-non-figurative, objective-nonobjective, geometrical-irregular, monochrome-polychrome, made forms-found forms, environmental-circumnavigable, big-little, and whatever other kinds one cares to sort out, there is already quite a smorgasbord to choose from. The fun really begins when two, three or more cross-combinations are made: monochrome figurative found-object environmental, say, or polychrome geometric nonobjective or geometric figurative, and so on.'

In the sculpture of today it is not only junk, automobile chassis, sheet-iron, old wooden crates, glass, paper, cloth and new consumers' articles that are used, but also traditional materials like wood, stone, marble and bronze, which have by no means lost their usefulness. Brancusi's work is a synthesis of traditional handicraft and new symbols of the twentieth century. The 'Endless Column' of 1918 (Pl. 165) is the prototype of a creation which combines the old and new spirits. Another example is the granite sculpture 'Yomon' (1962, Pl. 167) by Isamu Noguchi, a student of Brancusi's, which stems from an ancient tradition; Noguchi uses the material appropriate to that tradition. Other works by Noguchi, such as 'Two is One' (1964, Pl. 168), also made of granite, show the craftsmanlike brilliance of old Japan in this mastery of the material.

165 Constantin Brancusi *Endless Column*
1918

166 Naum Gabo *Construction in Space with Red* 1953

168 Isamu Noguchi *Two is One* 1964

170 Barbara Hepworth *Forms in Movement*

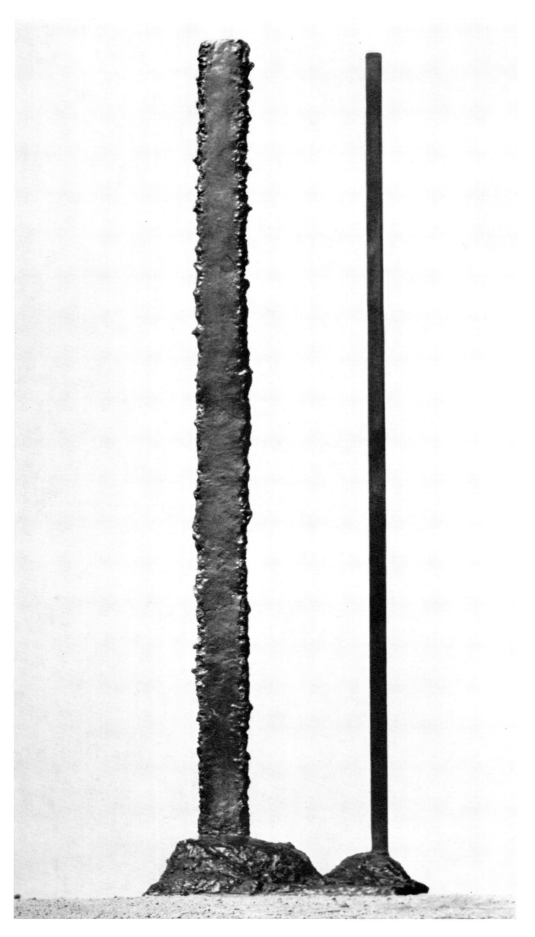

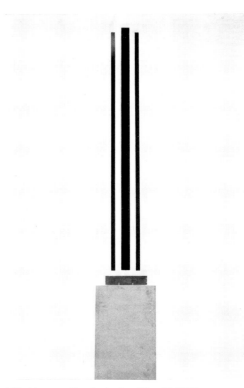

172 Nassos Daphnis *4 – J30 – 63* 1963

171 Barnett Newman *Here I* 1950

Right:
173 Barnett Newman *Here II* 1965

174 Lucio Fontana *Natura* 1959

175 Gottfried Honegger *Réciprocité I* 1961

176 Lucio Fontana *Natura* 1959

The sculpture of constructivism in all its variations has produced, in the works of Vantongerloo, Rodchenko, Tatlin, Pevsner (Pl. 241), Gabo (Pl. 166), Arp and Calder (Pls. 245–247), mere figurations which no doubt seem similar to Brancusi's pieces, but which testify in principle to a different attitude towards the world. They reflect the experience of the laws of the machine in modern production. Gabo's works are models of these new experiences and have been influential right up to the immediate present (Pl. 170). And yet we cannot overlook a new departure which originated around 1960. David Smith in the United States, especially with the involvement of space in the work of his last years (the 'Cubi' series since 1962), and Anthony Caro in England paved the way for these changes. Caro, who was a collaborator of Henry Moore's from 1951 to 1953, began with aggressive human figures, but from about 1960 he turned away increasingly from the traditions of expressionism and surrealism; with his large,

177 De Wain Valentine *Blue Tandem* 1966

Attillio Pierelli *Monumenti Inox* 1965

178 Attilio Pierelli *Struttura sonora* 1965
179 George Baker *Watcher* 1965   180 George Baker *Spiral* 1966

painted space-sculptures of steel and aluminium, he led the development of sculpture into a new phase. The young British sculptors were to a great extent formed by him, but since then they have decidedly rejected his model and have struck new paths. Even earlier there was Barnett Newman in the United States, whose steles made of steel were analogies to his exemplary spatial pictures. The verticals, in their extreme reduction, define a new space (Pls. 171 and 173). Lucio Fontana arrived from an entirely different basis at his 'Nature' or 'Concetti spaziale' (since 1959): balls made of clay or cast in bronze, with notches, holes, incisions, which likewise produce analogies to paintings (Pls. 174 and 176). Basic organic forms appear also in the works of George Baker, such as 'Globe' (1965) or 'Spiral' (1966, Pls. 179 and 180); the untitled bronzes of Edward Higgins (Pl. 182); the work done in the early 1960s by Andrea Cascella and emanating from new concepts, in which the moving parts seem to be hinged (Pl. 181). This is true also of John Wragg who, after such organoid pieces as 'Checkpoint' (1963), 'Unique' (1965) or 'Squeeze' (1965), has been making more austere,

Right:
182 Edward Higgins *Untitled* 1964
183 Ad Dekkers *Variatie op cirkels* 1965
184 Herbert Distel *Kegelplastik VII* 1965–1966

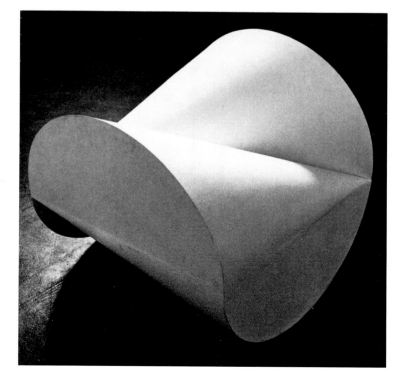

185 Robert Indiana *Love* 1966

Right:
186 George Sugarman *Two in One* 1966
187 George Sugarman *Inscape* 1964

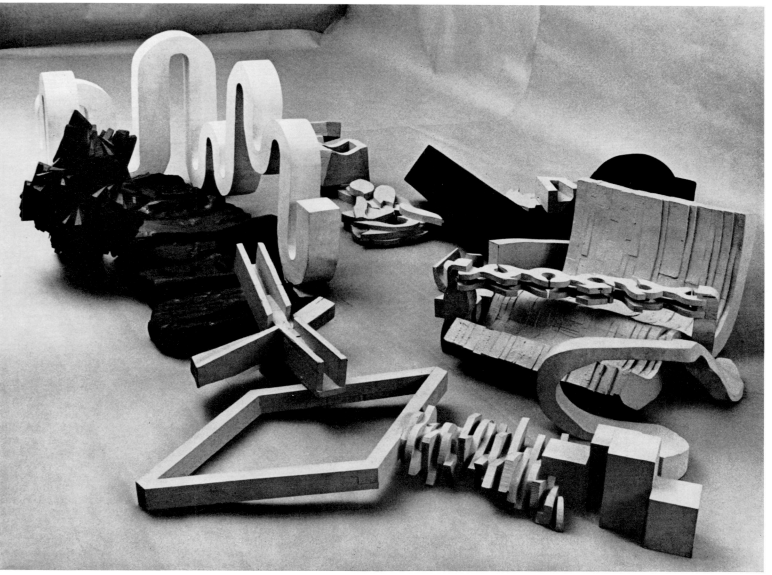

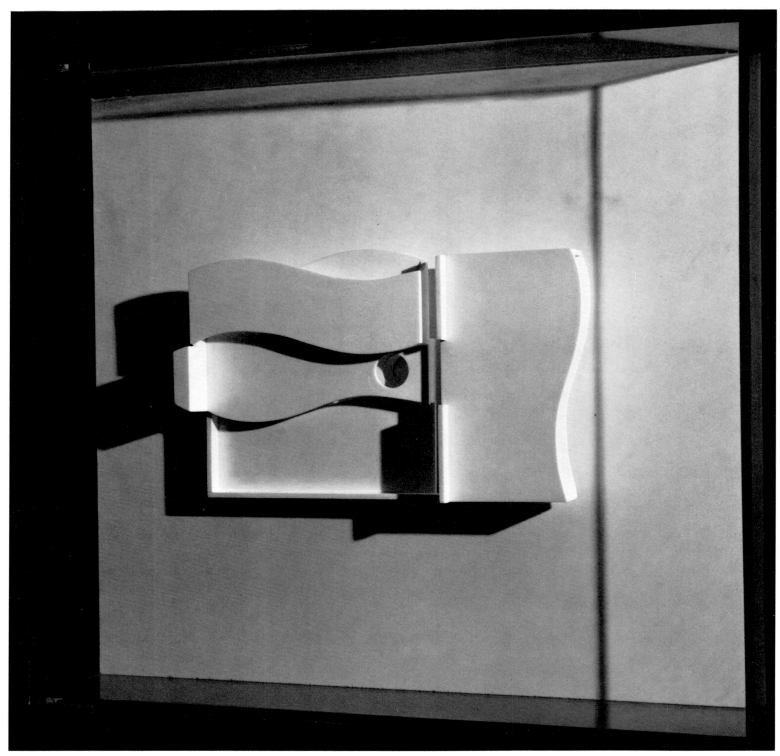

188 Eduardo Ramirez *Untitled* 1966

189 E. Negret *Mask* 1966

190 E. Negret *Mask A* 1966

spatially determined works like 'Place' and 'White Memory' since 1966 (Pl. 207). De Wain Valentine (Pl. 177), Herbert Distel (Pl. 184) and Ad Dekkers (Pl. 183) also seek an artistic union of movement and order, laws and freedom. In the steles of Gino Marotta ('Stele Solare', 1964), colour plays a large part in the effect. Robert Indiana, in his sculpture 'Love' (1966), as in his paintings, built the four letters of the word into a plastic ensemble (Pl. 185). In a similar way, the coloured ensembles of George Sugarman, developed out of prefabricated signs, are to be understood as plastic hieroglyphs (Pls. 186 and 187). The severe figurations of the South Americans, E. Negret and Eduardo Ramirez, are determined by the laws of the materials they use (Pls.188–190).

Eduardo Paolozzi, after his expressive figurations, created new works like 'Twisprac' (1966) or 'Durunmal' (1966), steel compositions covered with chrome, whose basic technoid forms recall Barnett Newman (Pl. 193). Alighiero Boetti (Pl. 195), Olitski (Pl. 194) and Lorenzo Piemonti (Pl. 192) constructed figurations out of tubes and flat surfaces which were similarly reduced to plain basic forms. In their effect they resemble the output, developed from a quite different point of departure, of the Paris group called Recherche d'art visuel, particularly the plexiglas sculpture of Francisco Sobrino. The sculptors Martha Boto (Pl. 315) and Gregorio Vardanega (Pls. 311–313), who belong to this group, as well as the Baschet brothers and Attilio Pierelli (Pls. 178 and VI), also incorporate a large measure of kinetic and acoustical elements into their sculpture. In the recent work of William Turnbull (Pl. 191), of the Czech sculptor, Karel Malich, and of the Italian, Carlo Lorenzetti, various types of basic forms are given imaginative expression.

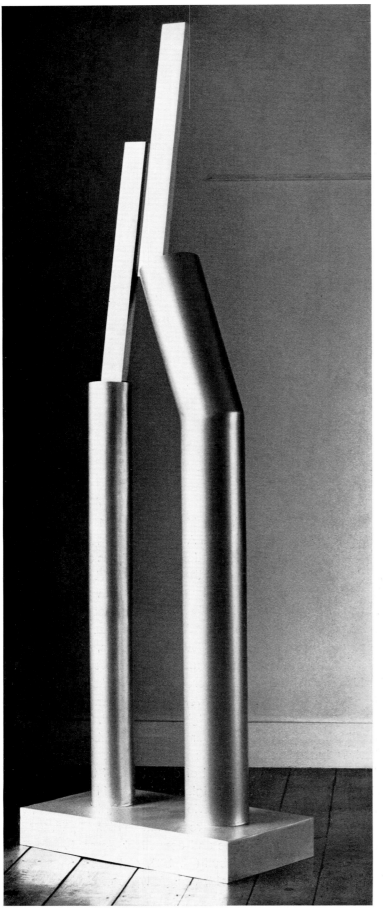
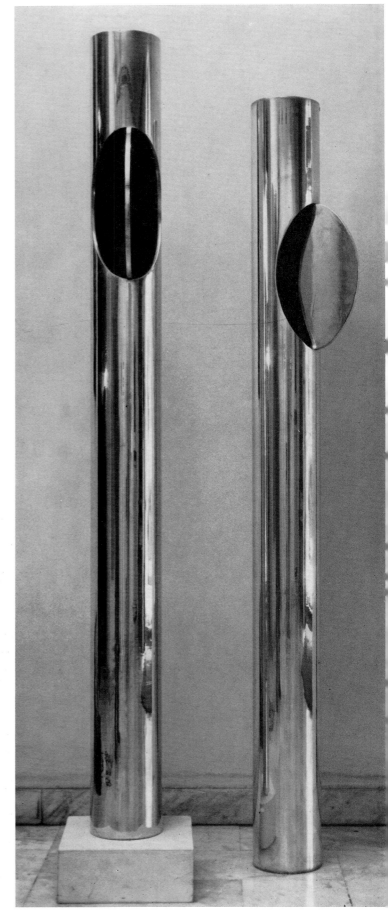

128

Artists are increasingly concerned with the spatial ramifications of their work. Many have gone over from painting to environmental objects, and to colour-space objects (Pfahler, Pl. 198; Lenk, Pl. 256; Kampmann, Pl. IX). Through the use of light and colour, Nicolas Schöffer has given his partly moving sculptures, based on geometrical-technoid premises, characteristics related to Happenings (Pls. 318 and 319). This is true also of the demonstrations of the Zero group and the Recherche d'art visuel in Paris. All of them strive for a synthesis of space, plane, body, volume, light and movement; and this corresponds to the 'material actions' in Vienna and Happenings in New York which emerge from a completely different direction.

While Newman's work already revealed themes tending towards the mystical and a new spatial experience related to those themes (Pls. 171 and 173), these features have become dominant in the developments of recent years. So-called environmental art is the determining factor in contemporary art. Among the forerunners in Europe are the Italian, Francesco Lo Savio, and the Pole, Voyciech Fangor, both of whom pressed beyond the regions of sculpture and painting in their quest for new spatial contexts. Lo Savio developed these already before 1960 from the laws of light, and wanted to attain a new arrangement on an urban basis (Pl. 200). Fangor seeks an experience of reality, which develops out of colour and the movement of colour into spatial forms (Pls. 330–332).

193 Eduardo Paolozzi *Durunmal* 1966

194 Jules Olitski *Sculpture I* 1967

195 Alighiero Boetti *Senza titolo* 1966

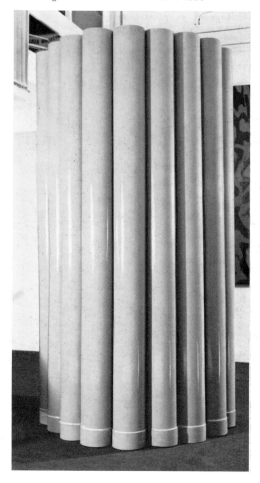

196 George Rickey *Four Planes Hanging* 1966

197 John Berry *Untitled* 1966

198 Karl Georg Pfahler *Farbraumobjekt Nr. 6*
1965–1966

The exhibition 'Primary Structures', mounted by Kynaston McShine in 1966 at the Jewish Museum in New York, was restricted to American and British artists, but it made public the fact that a great many artists were preoccupied with these efforts. In this exhibition the eye was especially struck by the space-structures of Robert Morris (Pls. 201 and 202) and Donald Judd (Pls. 203 and 204), and by the coloured space-sculptures of Phillip King (Pls. 218, 219 and XI), William Tucker (Pl. 216) and Peter Phillips (Pl. VIII). The effective media of this new space art transcend the laws of sculpture as much as they do those of painting. Further prominent examples were the works of Larry Bell (Pl. 226), Sol Lewitt (Pls. 234 and 235) and Dan Flavin (Pls. 325–327). In the catalogue, McShine forestalled the attempts of many critics to label the works in this exhibition as 'minimal art' or 'cool art': 'Most of these works contain irony, paradox, mystery, ambiguity, even wit, as well as formal beauty, qualities which have always been considered positive values in art.'

Tony Smith, who turned from painting to sculpture around 1960, and who has also done architectural work, would like to create huge monumental figurations in public places (Pls. 210 and 211). Ronald Bladen has also worked along these lines (Pls. 208 and 209). These works are examples of the tendency in both painting and sculpture towards large formats, going beyond 'gallery art'. John McCracken, too, has made large, mostly monochrome volumes since 1965; their space-colour presence opens up new aspects of our relations to reality (Pl. 224). Judy Gerowitz, Douglas Huebler, Paul Frazier, Richard van Buren, Peter Pinchbeck, Tina Matkovic and Clark Murray are only a few of the many artists inclining towards these new tasks. What their work has in common are large plain volumes, the use of colour mainly in aggressive intensity, and a consciousness of space which inevitably incorporates them into an urban context. Other artists who work towards an expansion of the sculptural vocabulary, along the lines of Primary Structures, are Anne Truitt (Pl. 215), Robert Breer (Pl. 351), Robert Grosvenor (Pl. VIII), Bonies (Pls. 212 and 213)—to name only a few.

199 Charlotte Posenenske *Ohne Titel* 1967

200 Francesco Lo Savio *Spazio Luce* 1959–1960

201 Robert Morris *Untitled* 1965

202 Robert Morris *Untitled* 1966

204 Donald Judd *Untitled* 1965

206 Michael Bolus *Untitled* 1965

Peter Phillips *Tricurvular II* 1966–67

138

Left:
208 Ronald Bladen *Black Triangle* 1966
209 Ronald Bladen *Untitled* 1965

210 Anthony Smith *Amaryllis* 1965

211 Anthony Smith *Playground* 1966

140

214 Robert Grosvenor *Tenerife* 1966

Left:
12 Bonies *Untitled* 1966
13 Bonies *Blauw-Rood-Geel* 1966–1967

215 Anne Truitt *Summer Run* 1964

216 William Tucker *Meru II* 1964–1965

217 Garth Evans *Rosebed* 1965

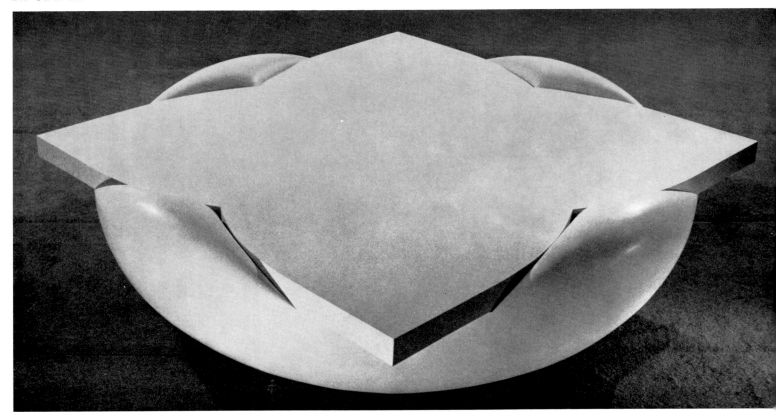

218 Phillip King *Genghis Khan* 1963

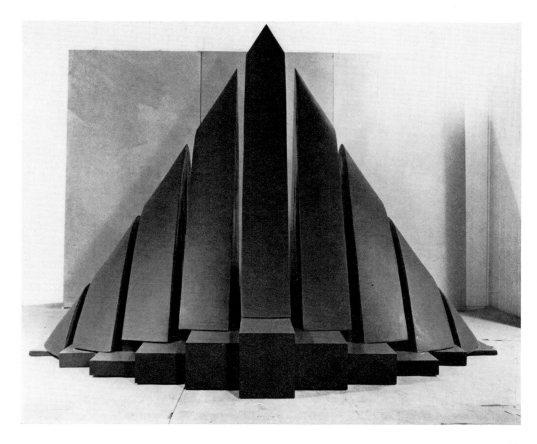

219 Phillip King *Through* 1965

220 Skidmore, Owings and Merrill
Sun Telescope, Kitt Peak, Arizona 1962

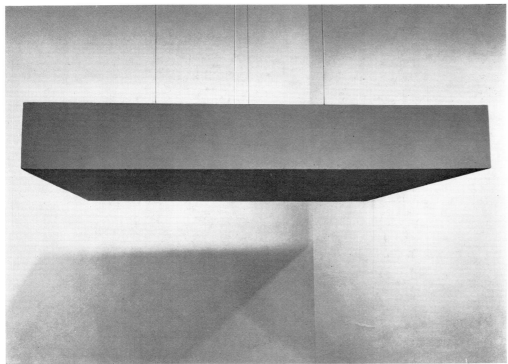

221 Robert Morris *Slab* 1962

Robert Grosvenor *Tapanga* 1965

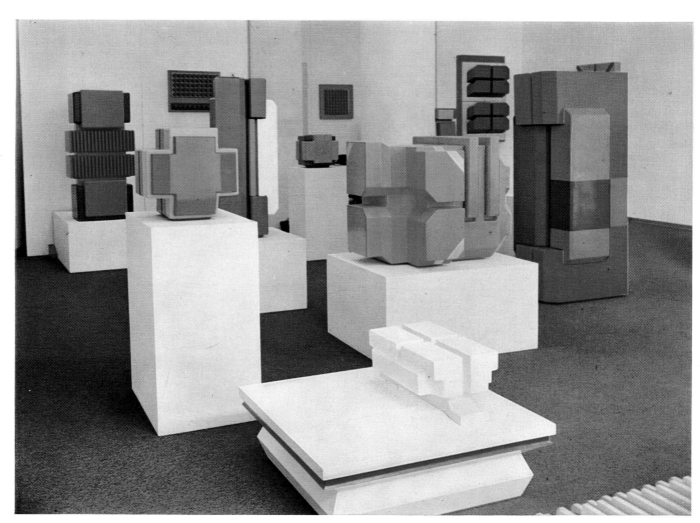

Rüdiger-Utz Kampmann *Exposition Zürich*
1966

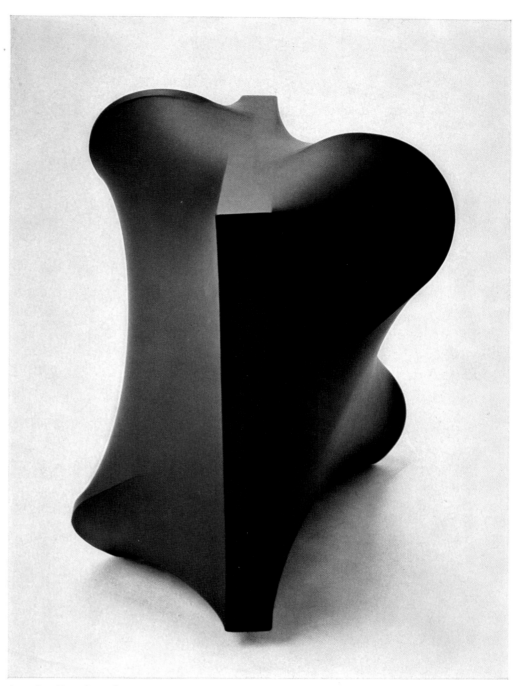

Agostino Bonalumi *Senza titolo* 1967

Phillip King *Slit* 1965

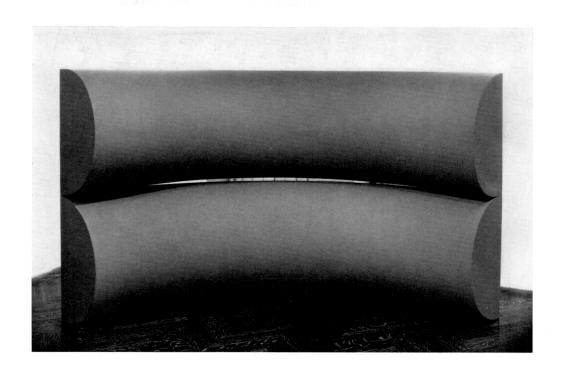

223 David Hall *Duo II* 1966

Right:
226 Larry Bell *Untitled* 1965

224 John McCracken *Violet Block in Two Part.*
1966
225 Alighiero Boetti *Senza titolo* 1966

227 Robert Morris *Exhibition Los Angeles* 1966
228 Gary Kuehn *Untitled* 1966

Right:
229 Michael Steiner *Untitled* 1965
230 David Novros *6:36* 1966

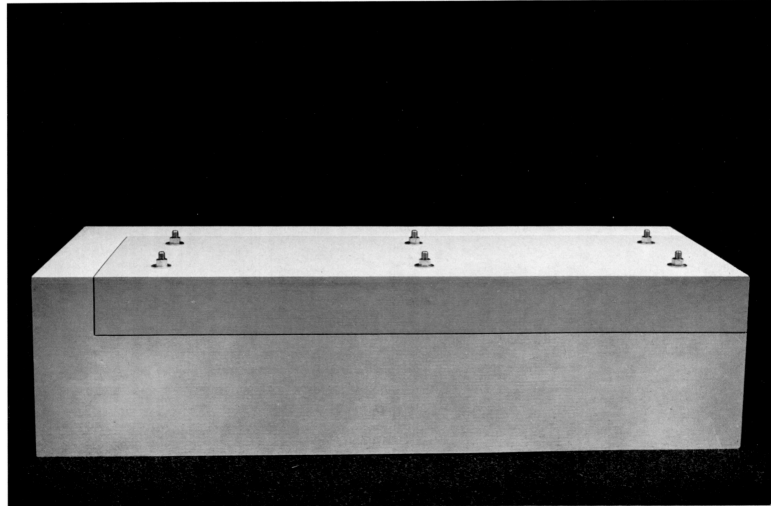

231 Kenneth Snelson *Audrey I* 1966 and
Audrey II 1966
232 Kenneth Snelson *Spring Street* 1964

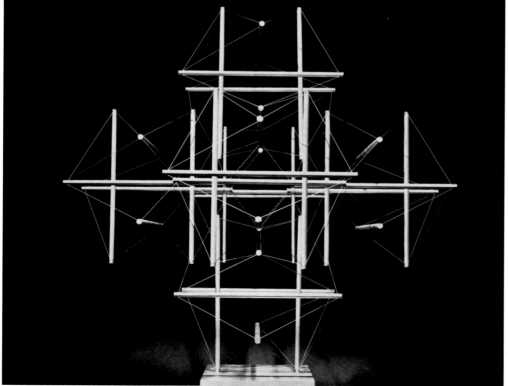

Right:
233 Peter Forakis *Outline* 1966
234 Sol Lewitt *Hanging Modular Structure*
1966

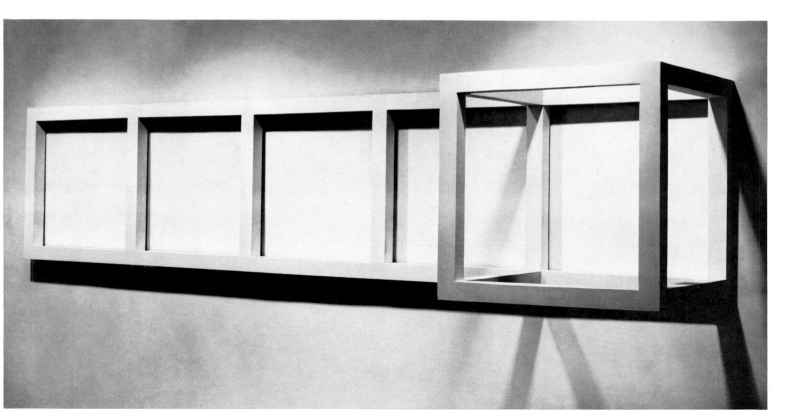

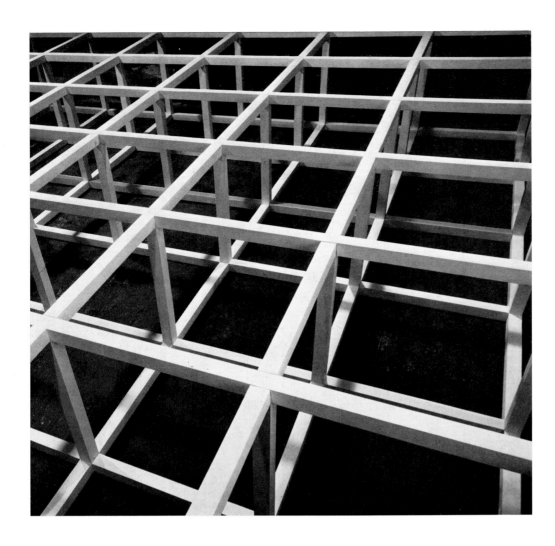

The result of these efforts is a search for synthesis. The symbolic rooms, for example, of artists like Yayoi Kusama ('Endless Love Room', Pl. 341), Lucas Samaras ('Room 2', Pls. 343 and 344), the Argentine artists around Marta Minujin ('Environment La Menesunda' in Buenos Aires), Davide Boriani ('Stroboscopic Room') or Christo ('Store Fronts'), have introduced new complexes of meaning into this art form, which would appear to be so non-symbolic. This art relates to the past as well as to the future. It has analogies with the three 'Merzbauten' of Kurt Schwitters (Pl. 333) and the environments done by Clarence Schmidt in the 1930s. Its forebears include the Watts Towers in Los Angeles, fashioned after many years of meticulous labour by Simon Rodia into a total work of art which combines space, colour and line. Whether it is a matter of public commissions or altering a room, this art is not directed towards the limited and peripheral decoration of buildings, but seeks to encompass architecture itself. It would like to renew urbanism through the constructive arts—Francesco Lo Savio's projects have this aim. The sculptor Mathias Goeritz erected monuments in Mexico which establish urbanistic accents (Pls. 274–276). Francesco di Teana has made plans for a university town (Pl. 277), and Christo wants to wrap whole buildings (Pl. 278). All these ideas are by no means speculative or absurd. The society of the future demands solutions, imaginative and economical at the same time, such as the young Japanese have already envisaged.

Yayoi Kusama *Endless Love Room* 1965–66

In its relations to architecture, the new sculpture differs from the old, though up to now there have been only few achievements in which this has been made clear. For some time now monuments and memorials, though many have been produced, have lost their inner meaning. 'Monuments are landmarks in which men create symbols of their ideals, aims and actions. Their purpose is to outlast the epoch in which they are created, and present a legacy to future generations. They are a connecting link between past and future.' These sentences come from a manifesto written in New York in 1943 and signed by J. L. Sert, Fernand Léger and Siegfried Giedion. This manifesto discusses the meaning of architectonic and plastic monuments of our time under nine points. Under Point 2 the authors say: 'Monuments are the expression of man's highest cultural needs. Monuments have to satisfy the people's eternal longings, and to turn their collective power into symbols. Truly living monuments are those which express this collective power.'

It has become evident that the collective power of the people can no longer find its expression in the image of an individual. The age of statues and cemetery monuments is gone. Dictators, who brutally deny the present reality, tend to immortalize their petit-bourgeois personalities through colossal monuments of themselves. In spite of their pseudo-monumentality, however, such statues contain a grain of genuine monument-representation. They stand for the man portrayed, and when he is overthrown, they fall with him or in his place. Even from this negative point of view it becomes clear to what extent a monument has ritual reality and expresses collective emotions.

236 Walter Gropius *Monument* Weimar 1925

237 Antoni Gaudí *Casa Mila* Barcelona 1905–1910

238 Ossip Zadkine *Monument*, Rotterdam
1953–1954

239 Henry Laurens *Statue* Ciudad Universitaria Caracas
240 Hans Arp *Statue* Ciudad Universitaria Caracas
241 Antoine Pevsner *Sculpture* Ciudad Universitaria Caracas

242 Reg Butler *The Unknown Political Prisoner* 1953

243 J. Wallace Kelly *The Unknown Political Prisoner* 1953
244 Herbert Ferber *The Unknown Political Prisoner* 1953
245 Alexander Calder *The Unknown Political Prisoner* 1953

Up to the French Revolution, monuments were almost exclusively dedicated to prince-ly rulers and generals, seldom to artists or scientists. In accordance with the social order, those in power represented the community. At the beginning of the nineteenth century, however, a basic change was initiated. And in the second half of the century, artists had arrived at the collective theme of the unknown soldier. The monument of our time—and most of all the memorial—is formed by the common people's percep-tion of life. In 1925 Walter Gropius created a monument in Weimar (Pl. 236). In his iron sculpture 'Montserrat' (1937), Julio Gonzales was still able to use the idea of a human figure—a peasant woman. In his monument for demolished Rotterdam, 'The Ruined City' of 1953, Ossip Zadkine represented a broken body, in accordance with his theme (Pl. 238). In 1945 Antoine Pevsner was moved to create a symbol of triumph: a power-ful V-form composed of many raised hands making the V-for-victory sign. Even this memorial, one of the few positive examples of modern monument sculpture, seems today an outdated expression of a specific situation. It was installed at the General

246 Alexander Calder *Mobile* Ciudad Univer sitaria Caracas
247 Alexander Calder *Interior of Aula Magna* Ciudad Universitaria Caracas. Architect, Carlos Raul Villanueva. Acoustics by Robert Newman. Sculpture by Alexander Calder.

248 Henry Moore *Working Model for Time/Life Screen,* Time/Life Building, Bond Street, London 1952
249 Henry Moore *Time/ Life Screen* 1952

Motors Technical Center in Detroit under a different name. A variant of it is in the University City of Caracas (Pl. 241), where there are also works by Arp (Pl. 240), Laurens (Pl. 239) and Calder (Pls. 246 and 247).

The 1953 world competition in England for a monument to the unknown political prisoner brought symptomatic results similar to those of competitions in other countries. The models entered from all over the world reflected the social and artistic splintering of the times. Works by sculptors such as Richard Lippold, Wharton Esherik, Keith Monroe, Herbert Ferber (Pl. 244), J. Wallace Kelly (Pl. 243) and Alexander Calder (Pl. 245) may be cited here as negative examples, notwithstanding the qualitative differences among the participating artists. The designs of important pioneers stood next to plastic illustrations of the theme and irrelevant pseudo-avant garde pieces. Reg Butler, awarded the First Prize, had originally incorporated human figures into his composition, yet they were subordinated to a dominating construction resembling concentration camp watch-towers (Pl. 242).

157

As in Classical times, architects rather than sculptors are nowadays drawn into the creation of monuments; and in other types of memorials as well, our times approach the aims of Classicism. One need only think of the favourite elements of expression in the Classical period: obelisks, pillars, pyramids, triumphal arches. In the 1920s Walter Gropius and Ludwig Mies van der Rohe gave early examples of a new conception of the monument. Eero Saarinen designed the steel arch of the Jefferson Memorial in St Louis in 1948. Le Corbusier's open hand monument in the new capital of East Punjab, Chandigarh (Pl. 56), accentuates the artistic unity of the city plan. Kenzo Tange's monumental arch in the Peace Centre of Hiroshima is a complete architectonic and plastic expression. This archway is not an isolated monument, but the centrepoint of a district used for spiritual assembly (Pl. 250). Social reality, new conceptions of artistic creation, and the plastic-architectonic possibilities of expression stand here in balanced harmony.

Besides the majority of plastic solutions which reveal only the inability to deal with the task of creating monuments, there have also been attempts to attach plastic works to architecture, independently of their character as monument or memorial. Such was Henry Moore's screen, originally intended to have moving parts, for the Time-Life Building in London (1952, Pls. 248 and 249). Naum Gabo erected his large sculpture in Rotterdam in front of the Bijenkorf department store (Pl. 254).

Almost all the other sculptures erected in public places suffer from their lack of location, their lack of relationship to architecture and surroundings. The thesis of architecture as the mother of art, nurtured by the Bauhaus ideology, has resulted in architects' freeing themselves from added elements and leaving no room for the display of sculpture or painting. Naum Gabo wrote in 1938: 'We must avoid the mistakes of our predecessors, who regarded art merely as a trimming to architecture.' Even at that time Gabo indicated the need for the complete unity of both arts, and gave as examples the caryatids of the Erechtheum, the statue of Athena in the Parthenon, the sphinx vis-à-vis the pyramids, the frescoes of Pompeii, the icons in Byzantine churches and the sacred images in Gothic churches. Finally he demanded this kind of artistic unity in the public places of our own times. Regarding his own efforts in this direction he wrote in a letter: 'The simplest and clearest thing would be to give the masses a

250 Kenzo Tange *Monument* Hiroshima Peace Center

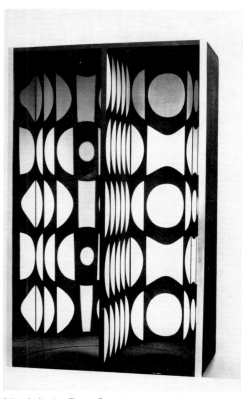

251 Julio Le Parc *Cerchi potenziali* 1965

252 Ettore Colla *Grande Spirale* 1962

253 Günter Uecker *Sculpture* Schalker
Gymnasium Gelsenkirchen 1965

254 Naum Gabo *Sculpture* Rotterdam De Bijenkorf 1954–1957

255 Christian Megert *Glass Sculptures* Landesausstellung Lausanne 1964

256 Kaspar-Thomas Lenk *Farb-Raum-Objekt 8* 1964–1965

257 J.J. Beljon *Hiroshima mon amour* 1964

chance to make their own judgments on this art. I am prepared to challenge any representative of public opinion, and to place any of my works he may choose where they belong—i.e., where the masses come and go, live and work. I would submit myself to any freely given judgment.'

Since those lines of 1944, the situation has not changed essentially. Architects are still sceptical of working together with sculptors and painters from the outset. It has been shown that limitations on works of art have lost their meaning and that considerations of space in all branches of art have been given new attention. For several years the Italian town, Spoleto, has made great efforts to display contemporary sculpture in the open. Also in Elblag, Poland, the most important native artists have worked together to create an 'open-air museum'. The Czech, Milan Dobes, has been able to incorporate works combining colour, light, space and movement into architectonic contexts (Pls.309, 310 and 316). In Italy the architect Paolo Portoghesi, the sculptor Cosimo

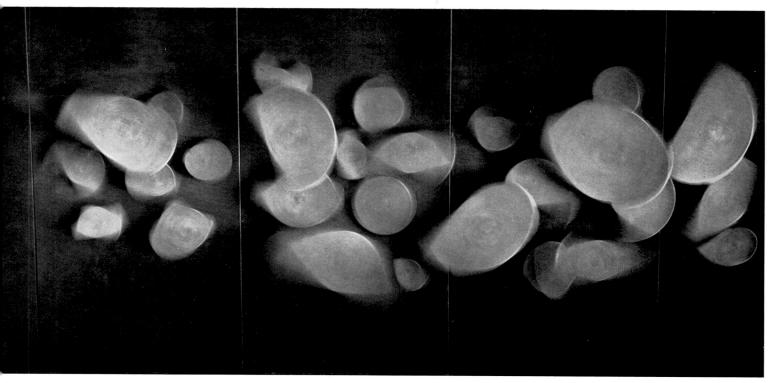

Left:
258 Vojin Bakič *Forme luminose 5* 1953–1964

259 Jean Tinguely *Wall* Studiotheater
Gelsenkirchen

261 Oskar Holweck *Mobile* Rechts- und
Wirtschaftswissenschaftliche Fakultät
der Universität Saarbrücken 1963–1964

260 Otto Piene *Façade* Cologne 1967

Carlucci and the painter Marcolino Gandini have decided to collaborate in exhibitions (Parabola 66) and buildings. Up to now they have produced imaginative one-family houses and the Colonia Marina ENPAS in Cesenatico. Artists such as V. Fangor, W. Wittek and F. Strynkiewicz participated in the construction of the Warsaw Mokotov sports stadium. They did not display isolated works, but contributed according to their individual capabilities to the whole structural complex. In the case of the Gelsenkirchen Theater, the collaboration of the architects Ruhnau, Rave and von Hausen with the artists Yves Klein, Norbert Kricke, Jean Tinguely (Pl. 259), Robert Adams and Paul Dierkes began before the building was erected, so that the result is, at least partially, a successful integration of various disciplines. Similarly, Lucio Fontana has constructed illuminated ceilings in collaboration with architects, and Oskar Holweck created a mobile in the roof garden of the Law and Economics Faculty of the University of the Saar in Saarbrücken (Pl. 261).

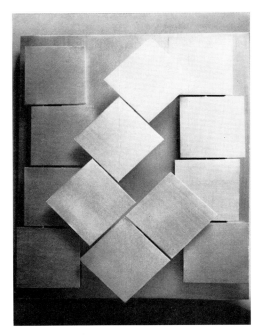

263 Louise Nevelson *Atmosphere and Environment I* 1966

262 Henryk Stazevsky *Rilievo 7* 1966

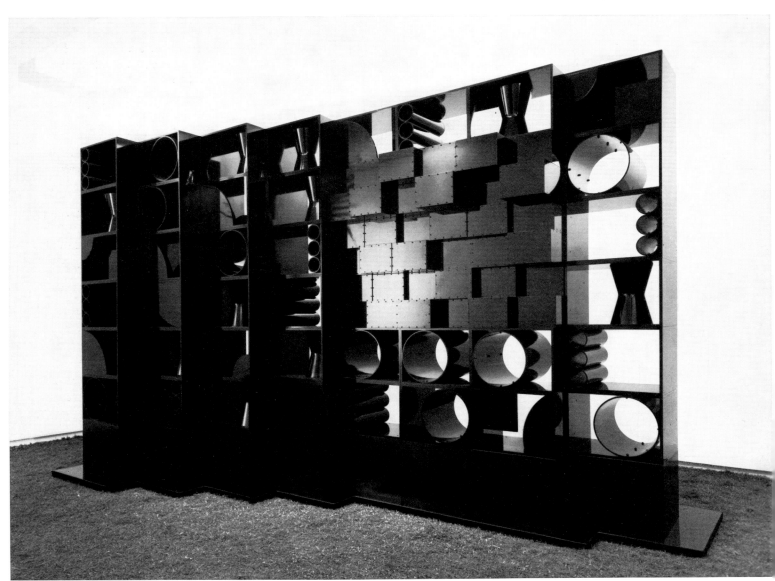

The free-standing outer wall, the wall joined to the building either inside or out, and the free-standing wall inside the room (screen), belong now, as formerly, to the most important tasks in the integration of sculpture. Relief-like wall constructions havebeen made, for example, by Kemeny, Adams, Paolozzi, Hajdu, Kricke, Stazevsky (Pl. 262), Demartini (Pl. 269) and Louise Nevelson (Pl. 263). These can be part of a total architectonic complex, if they find their independent place within the framework of an ensemble that demands them. Mathias Goeritz attempted a kind of plastic-architectonic poetry in his 'Golden Echo' of 1961 (Pl. 264): on the upper left section of a wall made of iron rings, he attached the word 'Oro' illuminated in red.

For a number of exhibitions the Paris group Recherche d'art visuel created large, partially moving relief walls with strong optical effects. The Swiss, Christian Megert, also made an effect at the 1964 Swiss State Exhibition with works of the same kind created out of glass, mirrors, light and movement (Pl. 255). Artists such as Ellsworth Kelly,

264 Mathias Goeritz *Golden Echo* 1961

266 Zdenek Sykora *White Structure* 1965

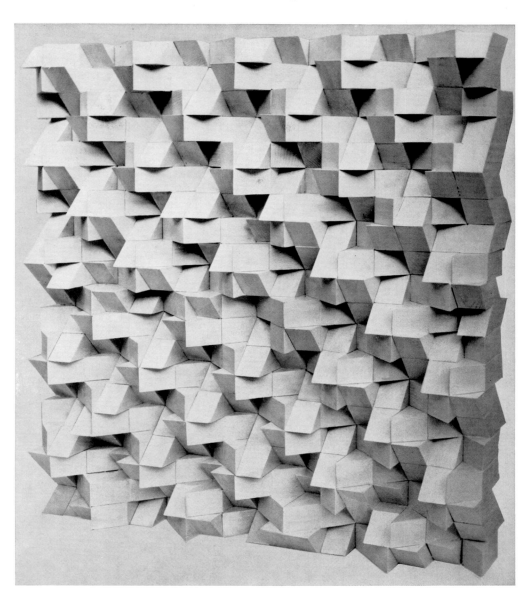

267 Paul Mount *Decorative Screen* Accra,
Ghana 1962

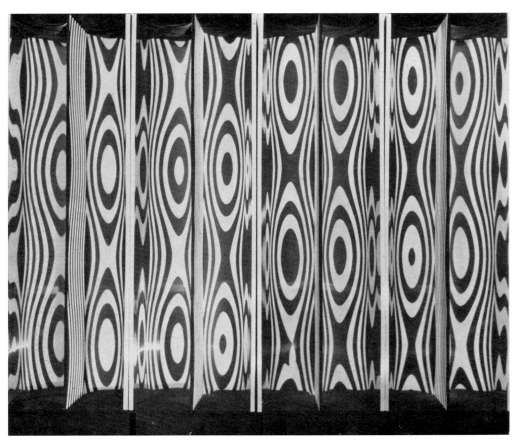

270 Julio le Parc *Grille* 1966

268 Julio le Parc *Courbes virtuelles* 1965

269 Hugo Demartini *Structure* 1965

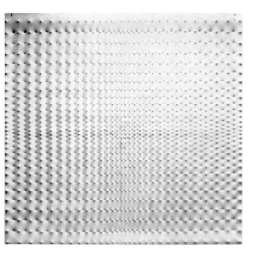

271 Enrico Castellani *Convergent Structure* 1966

272 Pino Pascali *Muro del sonno* 1966

273 Nanda Vigo *Unity of Habitation* with painting by Enrico Castellani 1966

James Rosenquist, Roy Lichtenstein, et al., collaborated with the architect and art collector, Philip Johnson, in designing the New York State Pavilion at the New York World's Fair of 1964–5. The interior designer Nanda Vigo has integrated works by Fontana and Castellani in her rooms (Pl. 273).

It becomes clear from these slowly developing trends that one is no longer concerned with mere decoration of buildings. The traditional basis of decoration was taken over from the cult buildings of the past. Gables, portals or capitals in temples and cathedrals were parts of the architecture with symbolic functions. It is an anachronism to carry over this conception to buildings which lack the same basis. New problems demand new solutions. Today all branches of art have outgrown their boundaries. They have burst through the framework of traditional distinctions and have moved into an area where architecture, sculpture and painting will have to meet under new definitions of meaning.

Half a century ago August Endell already said: 'All constructive art lives in space. It derives its effect from body or space.' A new universality is needed today, which does not exclude the traditional materials of artistic construction. Nevertheless new media have become important: light, space, water, movement. The creative artist of today no longer wants to present the world-picture in images or metaphors, but directly. He strives to connect the technical and the natural world with the spiritual world of man. Under different technical and social conditions, this has always been the impulse behind artistic creation.

274 Mathias Goeritz *Automex Towers*
1963–1964

275 Mathias Goeritz *Ciudad Satélite Towers*
Mexico 1957

276 Mathias Goeritz *El Eco* Mexico-City
1952–1953

277 Francesco Marino di Teana *Centre Universitaire* 1962

278 Christo *Edifice Public Empaqueté* 1960

The forces of the elements—water, air, light, natural (magnetism) and technically-produced energy—have assumed increased importance in present-day sculpture. Here, too, there is a search for sources and bases, and a rediscovery of the simple materials of nature which have long been left unused. Fire and light are introduced into the region of art, just as much as magnetic forces and electrical processes. These materials expand the artistic horizon in a way that is analogous to space-travel and the technology of rockets, for these also have their roots in artistic and poetic visions that are centuries old.

Today many artists have become interested again in waterworks. Following the grandiose and virtually exhaustive elaboration of water in the Villa d'Este, there was a movement again in world exhibitions of the nineteenth and twentieth centuries towards large-scale water constructions. The water-palace erected by Edmond Coignet for the 1900 World's Fair in Paris, besides being one of the first buildings made of concrete, fascinated the visitor with its orchestrated use of falling and leaping water. The writer Paul Scheerbart described water-palaces and water-sculpture in his visionary novels. In 1914, in the interior of his glass pavilion at the Werkbund Exhibition in Cologne, Bruno Taut combined effects of light and water in his 'light kaleidoscope'. Alexander Calder created a fountain in 1937 for a Spanish mercury factory. Jean Tinguely gained new potentialities from water in his various convulsively operating fountain-sculptures. Christian Megert works with a combination of moving panes of glass and water in search of an intensified unity of the effect of materials that reflect and are reflected simultaneously (Pl. 285). In his 'Water Forest' in the Düsseldorf bank building, Norbert Kricke made the movement of water itself the theme; water flows constantly down the outside of plexiglas cylinders which become barely visible (Pl. 280). Hans Haacke (Pl. 284), Yutako Ohashi (Pl. 282), Piotr Kowalski, Hermann Goepfert and Peter Hoelzinger (Pl. 281), and Liliane Lijn (Pl. 279) also seek in various ways to give moving

279 Liliane Lijn *Liquid Reflections* 1966–1967

water itself an artistic effect. Floating sculpture is only in its beginnings, although many unexploited potentialities exist in this field. David Medalla went to an extreme with his foam sculptures: foam is released from containers into the viewers' room and gradually fills the room (Pl. 299).

Another concern of artists with the energy of the elements is the use of air as a material. Piero Manzoni exhibited his work called 'Fiato d'artista' in 1960 (Pl. 291). The logical development was towards sculpture which was not tied to the ground; in 1965 Charles Frazier made 'Flying Sculptures'. In recent years Hans Haacke has made sailing forms (Pl. 295) and Christo his enormous bundles which are conveyed in the air by helicopters (Pls. 297 and 298). In 'Flying Vessels', Andy Warhol incorporated the reflecting effect of silvered surfaces (Pl. 294). Keith Sonnier's containers are based on the contrast between inflation and slackness (Pl. 296). These, then, are basic pneumatic forms, such as those Rodchenko already evolved in 1919, which play a special role in contemporary architecture (Frei Otto).

281 Hermann Goepfert – Peter Hoelzinger
Wassergarten Bundesgartenschau
Karlsruhe 1967

282 Yutaka Ohashi *Rain Box* 1965

283 Pino Pascali *Al muro: 1 metro cubo di terra, 2 metri cubo di terra; per terra: 12 metri quadri di pozzànghere* 1967

The numerous forms of so-called 'soft sculpture'—as developed above all by Claes Oldenburg—and the foam-rubber sculpture of artists such as John Chamberlain, Robert Israel (Pls. 302 and 303), Ferdinand Spindel (Pl. 335) and Ay-O, must also be placed in this category. These efforts run parallel with the use of air in pneumatic constructions for space-travel and architecture. Yutako Ohashi's 'Smoke Boxes' are comparable in aim to Medalla's foam-sculptures (Pl. 299). In 1964, Ohashi put three fragments of glass into a box and introduced draughts of smoke into the box which these fragments could direct, organize and structure (Pls. 286–288). Such works are on the border-line of Happenings. It is significant that in the most various types of demonstrations,

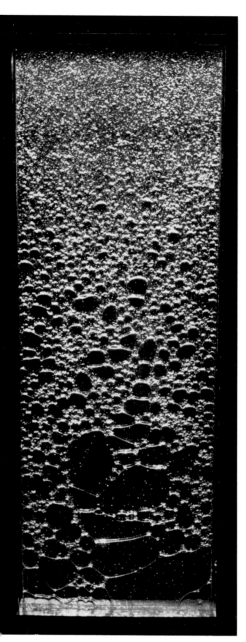

284 Hans Haacke *Brett Klar/Klar* 1965

285 Christian Megert *Fountain* Interlaken 1965

the effects of balloons and growing matter, smoke, water, light and movement have been put into use. In his 'Hanging Water Environment' of 1956, Sadamasa Motonaga gave water an anti-stable, mobile function. His Happening 'Growing', in the second Gutai Theatre Art (1958, Pl. 292), was built entirely around the theme of swelling and growing, as was Shozo Shimamoto's Happening No. 3 of 1957: 'Destruction of Object' (Pl. 293). Henk Peeters constructed a water ceiling in 1965, and Graham Stevens's 'Pneumatic Environment' in London (1966) was reminiscent of Motonaga. And Pino Pascali, carrying on his environment 'Il Mare' (Pl. 283), arrived at a direct incorporation of water.

89 Alain Jacquet *Grey Smoke* 1967
90 Alain Jacquet *Grey Smoke* 1967

91 Piero Manzoni *Fiato d'artista* 1960
92 Sadamasa Motonaga *Growing* 1958
93 Shozo Shimamoto *Destruction of Object* 1957

294 Andy Warhol *Exhibition* New York 1966

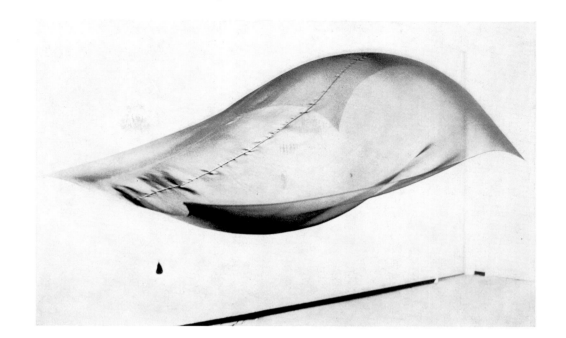

295 Hans Haacke *Segel* 1966

296 Keith Sonnier *Untitled* 1966

297 Christo *42390 Cubic Feet Empaquetage* 1966

There are manifold possibilities for the use of light in artistic construction. It cannot only be caught with the help of polished surfaces and mirrors—as Brancusi and, more recently, Vojin Bakič (Pl. 258) have done—but can also be transposed into movement as in Munari's 'Concavo-Convesso' (Pl. 308), where an unending movement in space is created. The Bauhaus already provided prototypes for an art using this element in the light-plays of Kurt Schwerdtfeger and Hirschfield-Mack as well as the sculpture of Moholy-Nagy. More recent trends can be seen in the work of Yaakov Agam, G. Kosice, Frank Malina, Abraham Palatnik and various groups of artists. The Argentinian, Julio Le Parc, seeks to bring light, movement, space, colour, the appearance of volume and people into relations which alter space (Pl. 270). The group of artists in Moscow called 'Dvizdyenye'—Nusberg, Akulinin, Diodorov, Galkin, Infanté, Krivchikov, Lopakov, Sapgir-Yanevskaya, Stepanov (Pl. 321) and Sherbakov—have likewise concentrated on the use of electric light to determine spatial effects.

Right:
298 Christo *42390 Cubic Feet Empaquetage* 1966

300 David Medalla *The First Sand Machine* 1964

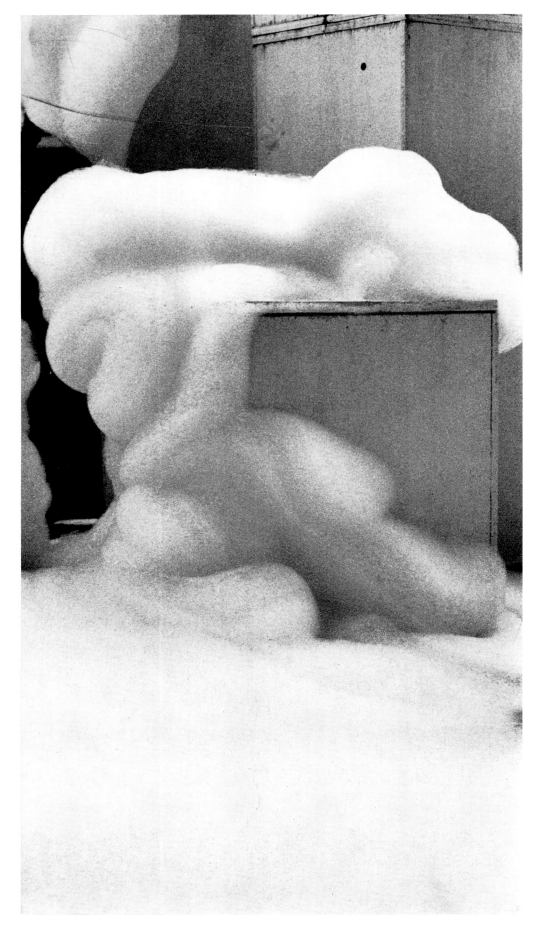

299 David Medalla *Cloud Canyons no. 2* 1964

301 Pino Pascali *1 metro cubo di terra* 1967

302 Robert Israel *Peach Progress* 1966

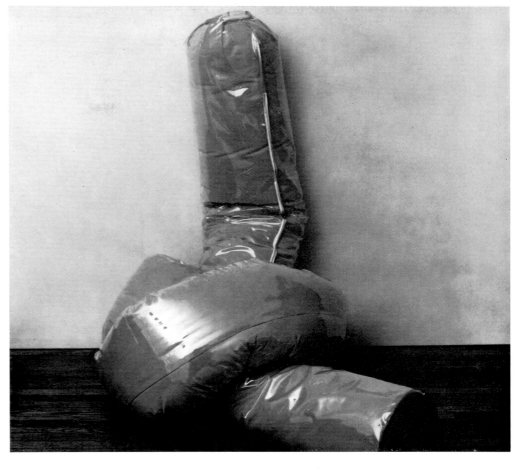

303 Robert Israel *Black Progress* 1966

305 Jannis Kounellis *Margherita con fuoco*
1967

304 Jannis Kounellis *Margherita con fuoco*
1967

306 Bernard Aubertin *Tableau-feu* 1965

307 Bernard Aubertin *Tableau-feu* 1961

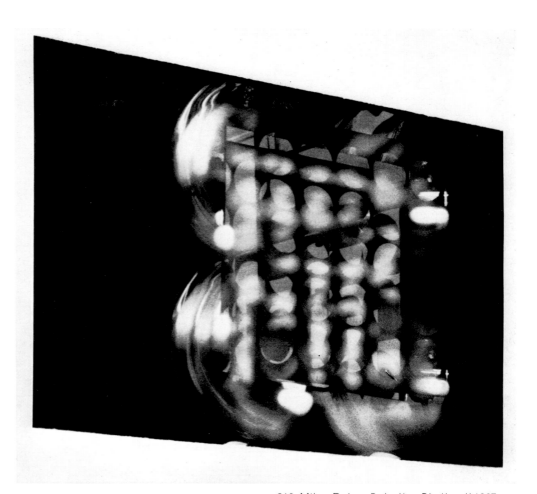

309 Milan Dobes *Pulsating Rhythm II* 1967

310 Milan Dobes *Pulsating Rhythm II* 1967

Left:
308 Bruno Munari *Concavo-Convesso* 1966

Whereas artists like Günter Uecker and Gerhard von Graevenitz have used concealed illumination as a device for the plastic structuring of their nailed or mounted relief-walls, others have more recently gone over increasingly to the creation of light-sculpture itself. Uecker's 'Light Rain' of 1966 is an environment composed of electric light, space and movement (Pl. 324). Lucio Fontana has created illuminated ceilings out of neon tubes for exhibition pavilions. Chryssa (Pls. 322 and 323) and Antonakos work with neon light. Robert Watts (Pl. 117) and Billy Apple use neon tubes for the intensification of their representative work. In a particularly radical way, Dan Flavin has composed spatial-constructive works out of shorter and longer neon tubes, whose main effect derives from the fluorescent light which changes the character of the space (Pls. 325–327). Some years ago, Nicolas Schöffer worked for a synthesis of light, colour, mechanical movement, music and dance in his spatial-dynamic or lumino-dynamic sculptures (Pls. 318 and 319). As Jean Tinguely has already done, Gregor Vardanega (Pls. 311–313) and Martha Boto (Pl. 315), Wen-Ying Tsai, Nam June Paik (Pl. 320) and Thomas Tadlock combine movement, light and sound. The movement of illuminated cylinders in Vardanega's light columns is synchronized with appropriate sounds.

In 1958 at the Morrison Planetarium in San Francisco, Belson and Henry gave demonstrations which combined optical, electrical and architectonic effects. In the same year Le Corbusier coordinated film, music and space in his 'Poème électronique', presented in the Philips Pavilion at the Brussels EXPO. Here too the attempt to create

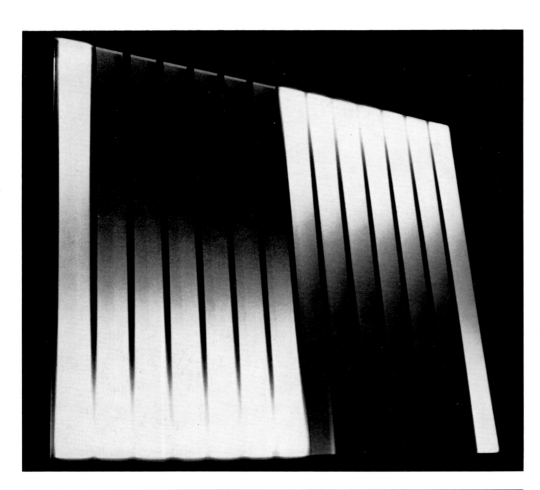

312 Gregorio Vardanega *Progression* 1967

13 Gregorio Vardanega *Couleurs Sonores III*
963–1966

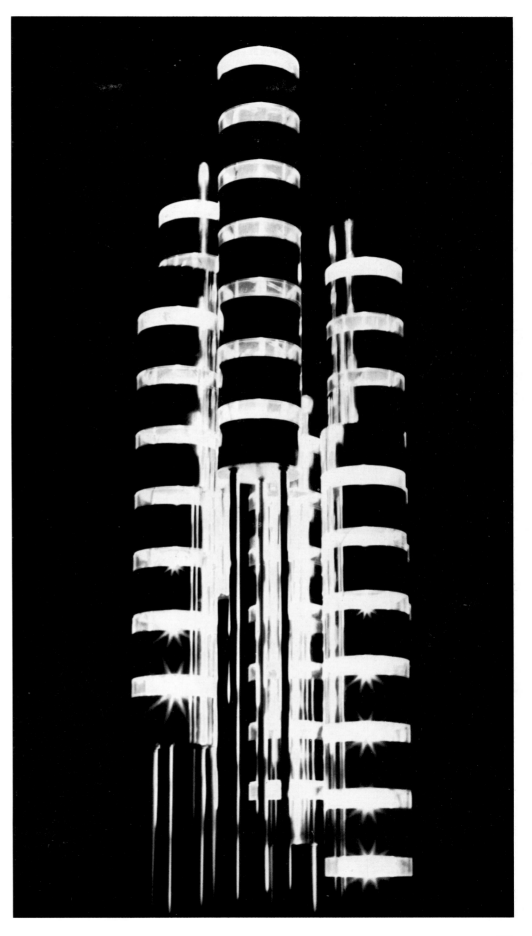

314 Demarco *Relief de placement continuel* 1966

315 Martha Boto *Mouvement helicoidal lumineux* 1967

316 Milan Dobes *White Lighthouse* 1967

317 Waki Zöllner *Mobiles Objekt* 1966

319 Nicolas Schöffer *Projections Lumino-dynamisme* 1958

20 Nam June Paik *Untitled* 1965

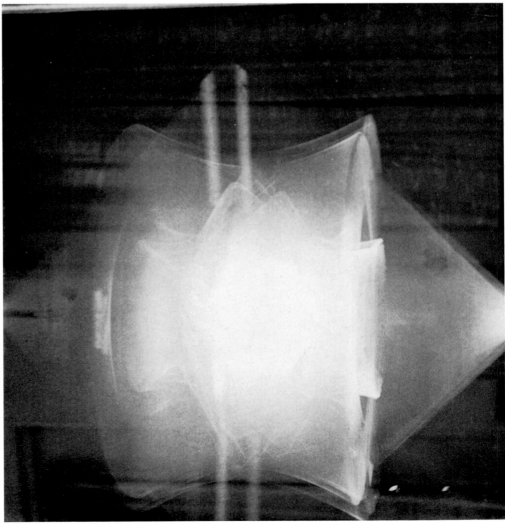

21 V.V. Stepanov *Mobile* 1966

195

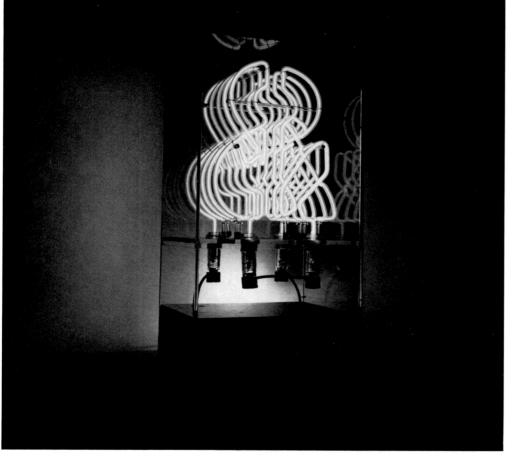

323 Chryssa *Ampersand V* 1965

324 Günter Uecker *Lichtregen* 1966

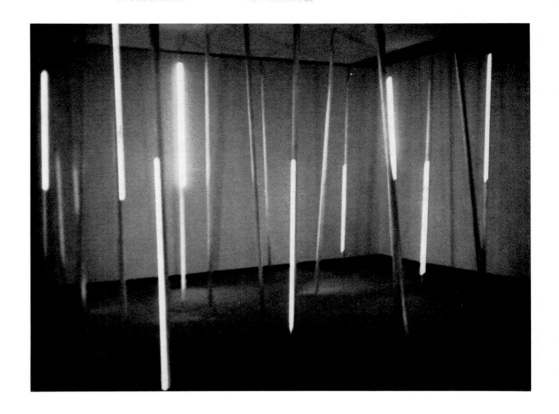

a synthesis of various categories is clear. The brothers François and Bernard Baschet have developed programmatic sound-structures, which are both bodies of sound and sculpture.

An extreme possibility for the involvement of the forces of the elements in art lies in the use of magnetic energy, which, because it cannot be made visible, can never be perceived in itself but only through its effects. Already in 1960, Davide Boriani used magnets as parts of his pictures. Gerhard von Graevenitz used magnets as the hidden impulse behind moving reliefs. In contrast, the Greek, Takis, experimented openly with magnetic force; he held specific forms in a state of suspension through the magnetic force of attraction. The heavy sculptures of the Venezuelan, Alberto Collie, are likewise suspended by means of magnetism. Nam June Paik uses electro-magnets from television-sets for his constructions and makes these electronic materials operate together in his works (Pl. 320).

From 13–23 October 1966, artists like Rauschenberg, Fahlström and Whitman, along with musicians (Cage, Tudor and Paik), dancers (Lucinda Childs and Deborah Hay) and radio, television and computer technicians (Wittnebert and Klüver), produced 'Nine Evenings-Theater and Engineering' at the New York Armory. The production, though not always convincing in its results, was nevertheless a pioneering event along the road towards a synthesis of the arts. The exhibition 'From Space to Environment' in the Matsuya Department Store in Tokyo (1967) demonstrated the high level of contemporary Japanese art.

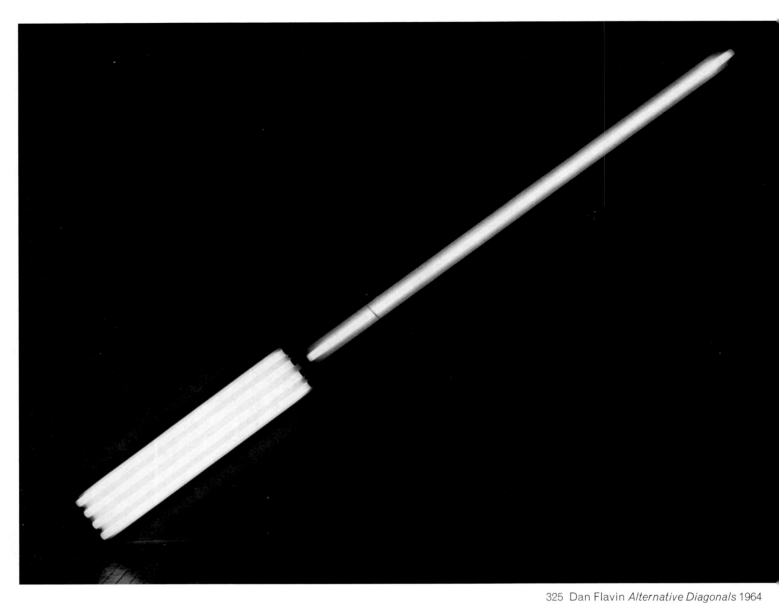

325 Dan Flavin *Alternative Diagonals* 1964

Right:
326 Dan Flavin *Pink out of a Corner*
327 Dan Flavin *Untitled* 1966

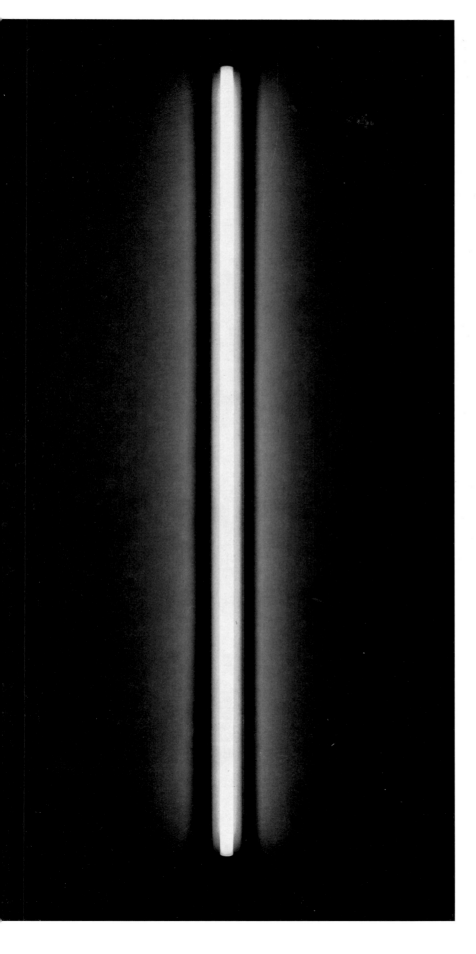
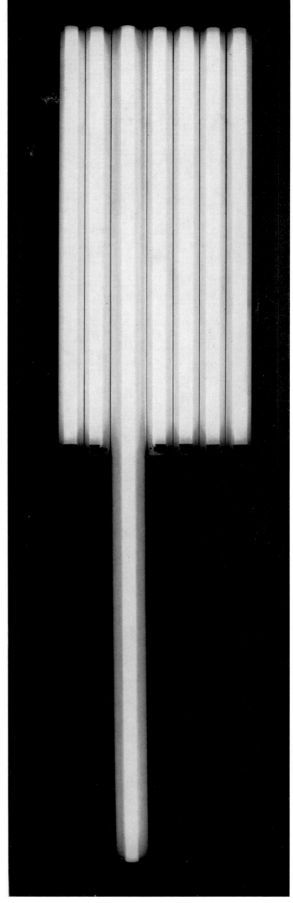

328 Martial Raysse *Promenade au clair de lune avec une fille de bonne famille* 1966

Right:
329 Martial Raysse *Proposition to Escape: Heart Garden* 1966

CONCLUSION

A survey of the heterogeneous tasks that contemporary sculptors set themselves clarifies the factors that distinguish this art from the past, and also the sources of its particular accents. Individual works of the past are viewed today in a new light, e.g., the 'Merzbau' of Kurt Schwitters (Pl. 333), Clarence Schmidt's environments, Simon Rodia's Watts Towers. These works, which were not understood for such a long time, were syntheses of space, equipment, significance, form, content, the imagination of the individual, collective urges and consumer reality. They reflect a world view which is concerned with overcoming the still-existing boundaries between those who create art and those for whom art is created.

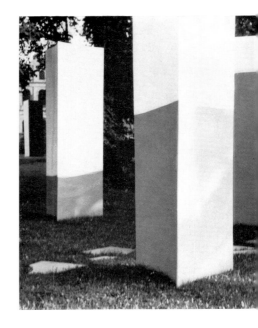

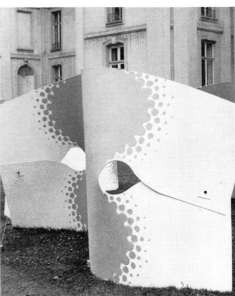

331 Voyciech Fangor *Untitled* 1961
332 Voyciech Fangor *Untitled* 1964

330 Voyciech Fangor *Untitled* 1959

202

333 Kurt Schwitters *Merzbau* Hannover

It is characteristic that in every category discussed here, one can observe a development from isolated to interrelated phenomena, from individual sculptures to environments—whether it is the human images of Arman, Segal, Marisol and Kienholz, the landscapes of Pascali and Marjorie Strider, the environments of Kusama, Samaras, Christo, Boriani, Gilardi, Minujin, or the urban visions of Borisowski, Constant, Friedman and others.

Finally, a few of the important achievements in environmental art should be pointed out. Martial Raysse adopted the phenomena of mass propaganda without qualms. For a long time he has done work in this field with changing, flowing, coloured light of a fluorescent effect. 'Raysse-Beach', 'Aurore IV' or 'Proposition to Escape: Heart Garden' of 1966 (Pls. 328 and 329) combine the most diverse media into a new poetic figurative cosmos. Equally significant are spatial constructions such as Kusama's 'Endless Love Room' (1965–6), a room intensified through mirrors and light into a boundless visionary reality which includes the viewer (Pl. 341), and Lucas Samaras' 'Room

334 *Yayoi Kusama's Studio* New York 1963

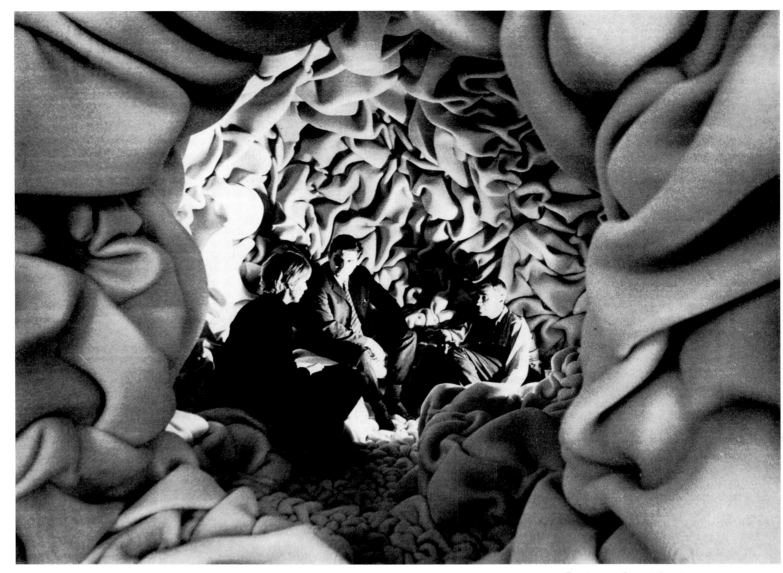

2', built of mirrors (1966, Pls. 343 and 344). There have also been significant joint under-
takings: the Happening 'La Menesunda' in Buenos Aires (1965), the 'Nine Evenings-
Theater and Engineering' in New York (1966), 'From Space to Environment' in Tokyo
(1967) and 'Lo spazio dell'immagine' at the Palazzo Trinci in Foligno (1967). In 1966
David Medalla outlined projects for environments, which reveal his aims but which
he has not yet been able to carry out: 'One of them is a project for a spatio-temporal-
tactile environment comprising of a swimming pool with submerged illumination, a
room with no gravity, and another room where the naked body will encounter, at ran-
dom intervals, showers of a resinous substance, and storms of silver and gold dust
accompanied by flares of light in different colours, and musical sounds. The gold and
silver dust will be imprinted in abstract patterns on the resin-soaked human skin.'

Right:
336 Paolo Scheggi *Intercamera plastica* 1967

204

38 Pino Pascali *Il mare* 1966

eft:
37 Mario Ceroli *Gabbia* 1967

340 Allan Kaprow *Happening The Forest*,
Yam Festival, Segal's Farm 1962

43 Lucas Samaras *Room 2* 1966

This development towards environment has been so prolific that it can no longer be overlooked. It is in part allied to the revived use of the elements as material and their incorporation into constructed contexts. Consumers' goods are taken over directly and introduced into structured spatial combinations according to new laws.

It is obvious that two tendencies are decisive, and they are opposed only in appearance. On the one hand there is the effort to define spatial situations by means of the extreme reduction of specific volumes or energies exposed to light; on the other hand, the effort to infuse real spatial situations with iconographic meaning. In many cases, the elementary, space-related composition approaching real events does not stop at city-space. Indeed, these efforts culminate in projects which, in the sense of a vision directed towards totality, seek to unify reality and illusion, life and art.

45 H.P. Alvermann

46 Arman

47 Ay-O

Artists' Biographies

Abrahams, Ivor
Born 1935 in Lancashire, England.
1962 Gallery One, London
1966 Grabowski Gallery, London
Pl. 19, 114

Accardi, Carla
Born in Trapani, Italy.
1960 and 1966 Galerie Notizie, Turin
1960 Galleria La Salita, Rome
1966 Galerie M. E. Thelen, Essen

Adam, Henri-Georges
Born 1904 in Paris; lives in Ville-du-Bois,
Seine-et-Oise.
1949 Galerie Maeght, Paris
1953 Biennale São Paulo

Adams, Robert
Born 1917 in Northampton, England; lives in
Hampstead.
1952 Biennale Venice
1957 Biennale São Paulo
1962 Biennale Venice

Adzak, Roy
Born 1927, lives in Paris
1965 Galerie Iris Clert, Paris

Aeschbacher, Hans
Born 1906 in Zürich; lives in Zürich

Agam, Yaakov
Born 1928 in Rishon-le-Zion, Israel; lives in
Paris.
1953 Galerie Craven, Paris
1955 and 1958 Galerie Denise René, Paris
1961 Licht Kunst Licht, Museum Eindhoven
1966 Marlborough-Gerson Gallery, New York

Agostini, Peter
Born 1913 in New York; lives in New York.
1960, 1962, 1963, 1964 and 1966 Stephen Radich Gallery, New York
Pl. 104

Alvermann, H.P.
Born 1931 in Düsseldorf; lives in Düsseldorf.
Pl. 20, 158, 345

Amen, Woody van
Born 1936 in Eindhoven; lives in Rotterdam.

Amino, Leo
Born 1911 in Formosa; lives in New York.
1940 Montross Gallery, New York

Andre, Carl
Born 1935 in Quincy, Mass.; lives in New
York.
1965, 1966 Tibor de Nagy Gallery, New York
1966 Primary Structures, Jewish Museum,
New York

Annesley, David
Born 1936 in London; lives in London.
1966 Waddington Galleries, London
Pl. 205

Antonakos, Stephen
Born 1926 in Greece; lives in New York.
1958 Avantgarde Gallery, New York
1964 Miami Museum of Modern Art
1966 Licht Kunst Licht, Museum Eindhoven

Apple, Billy
Born 1935 in Auckland, New Zealand; lives in
New York.
1963 Gallery One, London
1963 Institute of Contemporary Art, London
1965 Bianchini Gallery, New York

Arman (Armand Fernandez)
Born 1928 in Nice; lives in Nice.
1957 Galerie Iris Clert, Paris
1961 and 1963 Galleria Schwarz, Milan
1962 and 1963 Dwan Gallery, Los Angeles
1966 Galerie Ileana Sonnabend, Paris
1967 Galleria Sperone, Turin
Pl. 18, 23, 161, 346

Armitage, Kenneth
Born 1916 in Leeds, England; lives in London.
1946 Institute of Contemporary Art, London
1952 Galerie de France, Paris
1957 Biennale, São Paulo
Pl. 73

Arnold, Anne
Born 1925 in Melrose, Mass.; lives in New
York.

Arp, Hans
Born 1887 in Strasbourg; died 1966.
1954 Biennale Venice
1958 Museum of Modern Art, New York
1959 Museum Basel
Pl. 240

Artschwager, Richard
Born 1924 in Washington, D.C.; lives in New
York.
1965 Leo Castelli Gallery, New York

Aubertin, Bernard
Born in France; lives in Paris.
Pl. 306, 307

Ay-O
Born 1931 in Japan; lives in New York.
Pl. 347

Avramidis, Joannis
Born 1922 in Batum, USSR; lives in Vienna.
1956 and 1962 Biennale Venice
1967 Kestner-Gesellschaft, Hanover
1967 Galerie Appel und Fertsch, Frankfurt

Azuma, Kengiro
Born 1926 in Yamagata, Japan; lives in Milan.
1967 Galerie Senatore, Stuttgart

Baker, George
Born 1931 in Corsicana, Texas.
1960 Felix Landau Gallery, Los Angeles
Pl. 179, 180

Bakič, Vojin
Born 1915 in Bjelovar, Yugoslavia; lives in Zagreb.
Pl. 258

Bart, Robert
Born 1923 in Montreal, Canada; lives in New York.
1965 Leo Castelli Gallery, New York

Baschet, Bernard
Born 1917; lives in Paris.
1965 Licht und Bewegung, Kunsthalle Bern

Baschet, François
Born 1920; lives in Paris.
1965 Licht und Bewegung, Kunsthalle Bern

Beljon, J. J.
Lives in Holland.
Pl. 257

Bell, Larry
Born 1938 in Chicago; lives in Venice, California.
1962 Ferus Gallery, Los Angeles
1965 Pace Gallery, New York
Pl. 226

Bennett, John E.
Born 1935; lives in New York.
Pl. 160

Benton, Fletcher
Born 1931 in Jackson, Ohio; lives in San Francisco.

Béothy, Etienne
Born 1897 in Heves, Hungary.
1947 Galerie Denise René, Paris

Berlant, Tony
Born 1941 in New York; lives in Los Angeles.

Berni, Antonio
Born 1905 in Rosario, Argentina; lives in Buenos Aires.

Berns, Ben
Born 1936 in Ginneken, Holland; lives in New York.
1966 Licht Kunst Licht, Museum Eindhoven

Berry, John
Lives in England.
Pl. 197

Beuys, Josef
Born 1921 in Kleve, Germany; lives in Düsseldorf.
Pl. 118, 348

Biasi, Alberto
Born 1937 in Padua; lives in Padua.
1965 Licht und Bewegung, Kunsthalle Bern

Bill, Max
Born 1908 in Winterthur; lives in Zürich.
1953 Biennale, São Paulo
1959 Museum Schloß Morsbroich, Leverkusen

Bladen, Ronald
Born 1918 in Vancouver, Canada; lives in New York.
1958 Brata Gallery, New York
1966 Primary Structures, Jewish Museum, New York
1967 Fischbach Gallery, New York
Pl. 208, 209

Bodmer, Walter
Born 1903 in Basel; lives in Basel.

Boetti, Alighiero
Lives in Italy.
Pl. 195, 225

Bolus, Michael
Born 1934 in Capetown; lives in London.
Pl. 206

Bonalumi, Agostino
Born 1935 in Vimercate; lives in Milan.
1965 Galerie M. E. Thelen, Essen
1967 Bonino Gallery, New York
Pl. 349, X

348 Joseph Beuys

349 Agostino Bonalumi

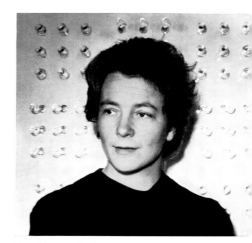

350 Martha Boto

351 Robert Breer

352 Mario Ceroli

Bonies
Born 1937 in the Hague; lives in Wassenaar.
Pl. 212, 213

Bontecou, Lee
Born 1931 in Providence, R.I.; lives in New York.
1960, 1962 and 1966 Leo Castelli Gallery, New York
1965 Galerie Ileana Sonnabend, Paris
Pl. 152, 153, 154

Boriani, Davide
Born 1936 in Milan; lives in Milan.

Boto, Martha
Born 1925 in Buenos Aires; lives in Paris.
1960 Salon d'art moderne, Buenos Aires
1965 Licht und Bewegung, Kunsthalle Bern
1966 Licht Kunst Licht, Museum Eindhoven
1967 Galerie M.E. Thelen, Essen
Pl. 315, 350

Boyce, Richard
Lives in England.
Pl. 16

Brancusi, Constantin
Born, 1876 in Pestisani, Rumania; died 1957 in Paris.
Pl. 47, 71, 165

Brandston, Howard
Born 1935 in Toronto, Canada; lives in New York.
1967 Lights in Orbit, Howard Wise Gallery, New York

Brauner, Victor
Born in Piatra-Naemtz, Rumania;
died 1966 in Paris

Brecht, George
Born 1926 in Halfway, Oregon; lives in Ville-franche-sur-Mer, France.
1967 Galleria Schwarz, Milan

Breder, Hans
Born 1936 in Westphalia; lives in Iowa City.

Breer, Robert
Born 1926 in Detroit; lives in New York.
1950–1955 Galerie Denise René, Paris
1965 and 1966 Bonino Gallery, New York
Pl. 351

Brusse, Mark
Born 1937 in Alkmaar; lives in Paris.

Buren, Richard van
Born 1937 in Syracuse, New York; lives in New York.

Bury, Pol
Born 1922 in Haine-St Pierre, Belgium; lives in Fontenay-aux-Roses.
1965 Licht und Bewegung, Kunsthalle Bern

Butler, Reg
Born 1913 in Buntingford, England; lives in Berkhampstead.
1949, 1954, 1957, 1960 Hanover Gallery, London
1953 First Prize in world competition for a monument to the unknown political prisoner
1952 and 1954 Biennale, Venice
1957 Biennale, São Paulo
Pl. 242

Calder, Alexander
Born 1898 in Philadelphia; lives in Roxbury, Conn.
1964 Solomon R. Guggenheim Museum, New York
1965 Musée d'art moderne, Paris
Pl. 245, 246, 247

Callery, Mary
Born 1903 in New York; lives in Huntington, L.I.
1955 Curt Valentin Gallery, New York

Camargo, Sergio de
Born 1930 in Rio de Janeiro.
Pl. 265

Cappello, Carmelo
Born 1912 in Perugia; lives in Milan.
1959 Galleria Schneider, Rome

Cardenas, Augustin
Born 1927 in Matanzas, Cuba; lives in Paris.
1955 One-man show in Havana

Carlucci, Cosimo
Born 1919 in San Michele Salentino; lives in Rome.
1964 Galleria L'Obelisco, Rome
1965 Centro Feltrinelli, Florence

Caro, Anthony
Born 1924 in London; lives in London.
1956 Galleria del Naviglio, Milan
1957 Gimpel Fils, London
1963 Whitechapel Art Gallery, London
1966 Andre Emmerich Gallery, New York

Cascella, Andrea
Born 1920 in Pescara; lives in Rome.
Pl. 181

Cassani, Nino
Born 1930 in Viggin; lives in Milan.

Cassen, Jackie
Born 1938 in New York; lives in New York.
1967 Lights in Orbit, Howard Wise Gallery,
New York

Castellani, Enrico
Born 1930 in Castelmass; lives in Milan.
Pl. 271

Cavaliere, Alik
Born 1926 in Rome; lives in Milan.
1951 Galleria Colonna, Milan
1967 Galleria Schwarz, Milan
Pl. 58

Ceroli, Mario
Born 1938 in Castelfrentano; lives in Rome.
1964 Galleria La Tartaruga, Rome
1967 Bonino Gallery, New York
Pl. 24, 25, 26, 27, 84, 337, 352

César (Baldaccini)
Born 1921 in Marseilles; lives in Paris.
1954 Galerie Durand, Paris
1967 Hanover Gallery, London
Pl. 6, 57, 75, 149

Chadwick, Lynn
Born 1914 in London; lives in Lypiatt Park,
Stroud, Gloucestershire.
1950 Gimpel Fils, London
1956 First Prize at the Biennale Venice
1961 Biennale São Paulo
Pl. 72

Chamberlain, John
Born 1927 in Rochester, Indiana; lives in New
York.
1957 Wells Street Gallery, Chicago
1960 Martha Jackson Gallery, New York
1964 Galerie Ileana Sonnabend, Paris
1964 Pasadena Art Museum
1967 Galerie Zwirner, Cologne
Pl. 147, 148

Chillida, Eduardo
Born 1924 in San Sebastian, Spain; lives in
San Sebastian.
1956 Galerie Maeght, Paris

Christen, Andreas
Born 1936 in Bubendorf near Basel; lives in
Zürich.
1964 Neue Tendenzen, Museum Schloß
Morsbroich, Leverkusen
1967 Biennale São Paulo

Christo
Born 1935 in Bulgaria; lives in New York.
Pl. 278, 297, 298, 353

Chryssa
Born 1933 in Athens; lives in New York.
1961 Betty Parsons Gallery, New York
1961 Guggenheim Museum, New York
1963 Museum of Modern Art, New York
1966 Pace Gallery, New York
Pl. 322, 323, 354

Cimiotti, Emil
Born 1927 in Göttingen; lives in Brunswick.

Clark, Lygia
Born 1920 in Belo Horizonte, Brazil; lives in
Rio de Janeiro.

Clarke, Geoffrey
Born 1924 in Derbyshire, England; lives in
Suffolk.
1952 Gimpel Fils, London
1952 Biennale Venice

Colla, Ettore
Born 1899 in Parma; lives in Rome.
1959 Galleria La Salita, Rome
Pl. 145, 252

Colombo, Gianni
Born 1937 in Milan; lives in Milan.
Member of Group T

Conner, Bruce
Born 1933 in McPherson, Kansas; lives in San
Francisco.
1958 East West Gallery, San Francisco
1964 Robert Fraser Gallery, London

Consagra, Pietro
Born 1920 in Mazara del Vallo; lives in Rome.
1947 Galleria Mola, Rom
1950 Biennale Venice
1956 Biennale Venice

Constant (Nieuwenhuys)
Born 1920 in Amsterdam; lives in Amsterdam.
1949 A founder of the Cobra group
1952 Biennale Venice
1956 Biennale Venice

Corberó, Xavier
Born 1935 in Barcelona;
lives in Esplugas de Llobregat.

Cornell, Joseph
Born 1904 in New York; lives in Flushing, L.I.
1966 Pasadena Art Museum
Pl. 81, 95, 138

353 Christo

354 Chryssa

355 Milan Dobes

56 Pieter Engels

Costa, Toni
Born 1935 in Padua; lives in Padua.
1960 A founder of Group N in Padua

Cousins, Harold
Born 1916 in Washington, D.C.; lives in Paris.
1955 Galerie Creuze, Paris

Couzijn, Wessel
Born 1912 in Amsterdam; lives in Amsterdam.
1948 und 1954 Biennale Venice

Cremean, Robert
Born 1932 in Toledo, Ohio;
lives in Los Angeles.

Crippa, Roberto
Born 1921 in Milan; lives in Milan.
1951 Alexander Iolas Gallery, New York
1960 Museum Schloß Morsbroich, Leverkusen

Dali, Salvador
Born 1904 in Figueras; lives in Port Lligat,
Spain.
Pl. 50

Dalwood, Hubert
Born 1924 in Bristol; lives in Leeds
1954 Gimpel Fils, London
1962 Biennale Venice

Daphnis, Nassos
Born in Greece; lives in USA.
Pl. 169, 172

Davidson, Michael John
Born 1939 in Maidenhead.
1967 Grabowski Gallery, London
Pl. 21, 22

Dekkers, Ad
Born 1938; lives in Amsterdam.
Pl. 183

De Lap, Tony
Born 1927 in Oakland, California; lives in Co-
rona del Mar, California.
1954 Richmond Art Center, California
1965 Robert Elkon Gallery, New York

Demarco, Hugo Rodolfo
Born 1932 in Buenos Aires; lives in Paris.
1961 Galerie Denise René, Paris
1964 Sidney Janis Gallery, New York
1964 Gimpel und Hanover, Zürich
Pl. 314

Demartini, Hugo
Lives in Prague.
Pl. 269

De Maria, Walter
Born 1935 in Albany, California; lives in New
York.
1967 Cordier and Eckström, New York

De Rivera, Jose
Born 1904 in West Baton Rouge; lives in New
York.

D'Haese, Roel
Born 1921 in Grammont, Belgium; lives in
Rhode-Saint-Genèse.

D'Haese, Reinhout
Born 1929 in Grammont, Belgium; lives in
Brussels.

Di Teana, Francesco Marino
Born 1920 in Teana, Italy; lives in Paris.
Pl. 277

Dietmann, Erik
Born 1937 in Jönköping; lives in Nice.
1966 Galerie Mathias Fels, Paris

Dine, Jim
Born 1935 in Cincinnati, Ohio; lives in New
York.
1959 and 1960 Judson Gallery, New York
1960 and 1961 Reuben Gallery, New York
1963 Sidney Janis Gallery, New York
Pl. 59, 94, 116

Distel, Herbert
Lives in Bern.
Pl. 184

Dobes, Milan
Born 1929 in Prerov, Czechoslovakia; lives in
Bratislava.
1965 Prague
1966 Licht Kunst Licht, Museum Eindhoven
Pl. 309, 310, 316, 355

Dodeigne, Eugène
Born 1923 in Rouvreux; lives in Bondues.

Doyle, Tom
Born 1928 in Jerry City, Ohio; lives in New
York.
1966 Dwan Gallery, New York

Duchamp, Marcel
Born 1887 in Blainville; lives in New York.

Duchamp-Villon, Raymond
Born 1876 in Damville; died 1918 in Cannes.

Durchanek, Ludvik
Born 1902 in Vienna; lives in New York.
1958, 1960, 1961 Graham Gallery, New York
Pl. 11

Dzamonya, Dusan
Born 1928 in Strumica, Yugoslavia; lives in Zagreb.
1954 Biennale Venice

Engels, Pieter
Lives in Amsterdam
Pl. 356

Ernst, Max
Born 1891 in Brühl; lives in Sedona, Arizona.
Pl. 2

Evans, Garth
Lives in England.
Pl. 217

Falkenstein, Claire
Born 1909 in San Francisco; lives in Paris.

Fangor, Voyciech
Born 1922 in Warsaw; lives in New York.
1964 Museum Schloß Morsbroich, Leverkusen
Pl. 330, 331, 332

Ferber, Herbert
Born 1906 in New York; lives in New York.
Pl. 244

Ferrant, Angel
Born 1891 in Madrid; lives in Madrid.

Flavin, Dan
Born 1933 in New York; lives in Cold Spring, New York.
1961 Judson Gallery, New York
1964 Kaymar Gallery, New York
1964 Green Gallery, New York
1966 Galerie Rudolf Zwirner, Cologne
1966 Nicholas Wilder Gallery, Los Angeles
Pl. 325, 326, 327

Fontana, Lucio
Born 1899 in Rosario, Argentina; lives in Milan.
1962 Museum Schloß Morsbroich, Leverkusen
1966 Walker Art Center, Minneapolis
1966 Licht Kunst Licht, Museum Eindhoven
Pl. 174, 176

Forakis, Peter
Born 1927 in Hanna, Wyoming; lives in New York.
1962 and 1964 Tibor de Nagy Gallery, New York
Pl. 233

Franchina, Nino
Born 1912 in Palmanova; lives in Rome.

Frazier, Charles
Born 1930 in Morris, Oklahoma; lives in Sea Cliffs, L.I.
1963 and 1965 Kornblee Gallery, New York
1965 Dwan Gallery, Los Angeles
Pl. 61, 62, 64, 78, 130

Frazier, Paul
Born 1922 in Ohio; lives in Flushing, L.I.

Frenken, Jaak
Born 1929 in s'Hertogenbosch; lives in s'Hertogenbosch.

Freundlich, Otto
Born 1878 in Stolp; died 1943 in Poland.

Gabo, Naum
Born 1890 in Bryansk; lives in Woodbury, Conn.
Pl. 166, 254

Gallo, Frank
Born 1933 in Toledo, Ohio; lives in Urbana, Ill.
1963, 1964 and 1965 Gilman Galleries, Chicago
1965 Graham Gallery, New York
Pl. 28, 29, 54

Gandini, Marcolini
Born 1937 in Rome; lives in Paris.

Garcia-Rossi, Horacio
Born 1929 in Buenos Aires; lives in Paris.

Garelli, Franco
Born 1909 in Diano d'Alba; lives in Turin.
1957 Galerie Rive Droite, Paris

Gargallo, Pablo
Born 1881 in Maella; died 1936

Gaudí, Antoni
Born 1852, died 1926.
Pls. 9, 122, 237.

Gentils, Vic
Born 1919 in England; lives in Antwerp.

Gerowitz, Judy
Born 1939 in Chicago; lives in Los Angeles.
1966 Rolf Nelson Gallery, Los Angeles

Giacometti, Alberto
Born 1901 in Stampa, Switzerland; died 1965 in Chur.
Pl. 4

Gilardi, Piero
Born 1942 in Turin; lives in Turin.
1966 Galleria Sperone, Turin
1967 Galerie Ileana Sonnabend, Paris
1967 Fischbach Gallery, New York
Pl. 102, III

Gilioli, Emilio
Born 1911 in Paris; lives in Paris.

Goepfert, Hermann
Born 1926 in Frankfurt; lives in Frankfurt.
1965 Licht und Bewegung, Kunsthalle Bern
1967 Bundesgartenschau Karlsruhe
Pl. 281

Goeritz, Mathias
Born 1915 in Danzig; lives in Cuernavaca, Mexico.
Pl. 264, 274, 275, 276

Gonzales, Julio
Born 1876 in Barcelona; died 1942 in Arceuil
Pl. 5

Goode, Joe
Born 1937 in Oklahoma; lives in Los Angeles.
1963 Dilexi Gallery, Los Angeles
1966 Nicholas Wilder Gallery, Los Angeles
1967 Rowan Gallery, London

Goodyear, John
Born 1930 in Southgate, California.
1964 Amel Gallery, New York

Gorski, Daniel
Born 1939 in Cleveland; lives in New York.

Graevenitz, Gerhard von
Born 1934 in Schilde, Germany; lives in Munich.
1962 Galerie Roepke, Wiesbaden
1965 and 1967 Galerie Klihm, München

Graham, Robert
Born 1938 in Mexico; lives in Los Angeles.
1965 and 1966 Nicholas Wilder Gallery, Los Angeles
1967 Galerie M. E. Thelen, Essen
Pl. 31, 32, 33, 34, 35, 136, I

Gray, David
Born 1927 in Waukesha, Wisconsin; lives in Costa Mesa, California.

Grosvenor, Robert
Born 1937 in New York; lives in Newport, R.I.
1967 Park Place Gallery, New York
Pl. 214, VIII

57 Gottfried Honegger

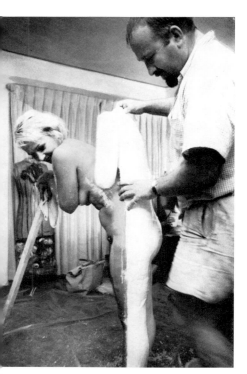

58 Edward Kienholz

Haacke, Hans
Born 1936 in Cologne; lives in New York.
1965 Licht und Bewegung, Kunsthalle Bern
Pl. 284, 295

Haber, Shamai
Born 1922; lives in Paris.
1960 Musée Bourdelle, Paris

Hajdu, Etienne
Born 1907 in Turda, Rumania; lives in
Bagneux.

Hall, David
Born 1937 in London; lives in London.
Pl. 223

Hare, David
Born 1917 in New York; lives in Roxbury,
Conn.

Harris, Paul
Born 1925 in Orlando; lives in Bolinas, California.
1960, 1963 and 1967 Poindexter Gallery, New
York

Hatchett, Duayne
Born 1925 in Shawnee; lives in Columbus,
Ohio.

Hausmann, Raoul
Born 1886 in Vienna; lives in Limoges, France.

Healey, John
Born 1894 in London; lives in London.
1964 Royal College of Art Galleries, London

Heerich, Erwin
Born 1922 in Cassel; lives in Düsseldorf.

Henderikse, Jan
Born 1937 in Delft; lives in Ottrabanda,
Curaçao.

Hepworth, Barbara
Born 1903 in Wakefield; lives in St Ives, Corn-
wall.
1950 Biennale Venice
1959 Biennale São Paulo
1954 and 1962 Whitechapel Art Gallery, London
Pl. 170

Higgins, Edward
Born 1930 in Gaffney, South Carolina;
lives in Easton, Pa.

Hiquily, Philippe
Born 1925 in Paris; lives in Paris.

Höke, Bernhard
Born 1939 in Brunswick; lives in Berlin.
Pl. 96, 124

Hoeydonck, Paul van
Born 1925 in Antwerp; lives in Antwerp.
1961 Palais des Beaux Arts, Brussels
1964 Galerie Iris Clert, Paris
1965 Galerie M. E. Thelen, Essen
Pl. 93, 97

Hoflehner, Rudolf
Born 1916 in Linz; lives in Vienna.

Hogle, Richard
Born 1939 in Brooklyn, N. Y.; lives in New
Paltz, N. Y.

Holmgren, Martin
Born 1924 in Ludviga, Sweden: lives in Stockholm.

Holweck, Oskar
Born 1924 in St Ingbert; lives in Saarbrücken.
1961 Museum Schloß Morsbroich, Leverkusen
Pl. 261

Honegger, Gottfried
Born 1917 in Zürich; lives in Paris and Zürich.
1960 Martha Jackson Gallery, New York
1963 Gimpel und Hanover, Zürich
1963 Galerie Lawrence, Paris
1965 Galerie M. E. Thelen, Essen
1967 Purchase Award, Pittsburgh Carnegie
Institute
Pl. 175, 357

Howard, Robert A.
Born 1922 in Sapulpa, Oklahoma; lives in
Chapel Hill, N. Carolina.

Hsiung, Ping-Ming
Born 1922 in Nanking; lives in Paris.

Icaro, Paolo
Born 1936 in Turin; lives in Rome.

Indiana, Robert
Born 1928 in New Castle, Indiana; lives in
New York.
1962, 1964 and 1966 Stable Gallery, New York
1966 Galerie Schmela, Düsseldorf
1966 Museum Eindhoven
1966 Museum Haus Lange, Krefeld
Pl. 185

Ipoustéguy, Jean
Born 1920 in Dun-sur-Meuse; lives in Choisy-
le-Roi.
Pl. 17

Israel, Robert
Born 1939 in USA.
Pl. 302, 303

Jacobsen, Robert
Born 1912 in Copenhagen; lives in Paris.

Jacquet, Alain
Born 1939 in Neuilly sur Seine; lives in Paris.
1966 Galerie M. E. Thelen, Essen
Pl. 38, 289, 290

Jeal, Douglas
Born 1944.
1966 Grabowski Gallery, London

Johns, Jasper
Born 1930 in Allendale, South Carolina; lives
in New York.
1958 Leo Castelli Gallery, New York
1959 Galerie Rive Droite, Paris
1962 Galerie Ileana Sonnabend, Paris
Pl. 67, 88

Jones, Howard
Born 1929; lives in St Louis, Missouri.
1965/66 Art Turned On, Institute of Contemporary Art, Boston

Jones, Joe
Born 1934; lives in New York.
1965/66 Art Turned On, Institute of Contemporary Art, Boston

Judd, Donald
Born 1928 in Excelsior Springs, Miss.; lives in
New York.
1965 Museum Stockholm
1966 Leo Castelli Gallery, New York
Pl. 203, 204

Kampmann, Rüdiger-Utz
Born 1935 in Berlin; lives in Zürich.
1965 Galerie Müller, Stuttgart
1966 City-Galerie, Zürich
Pl. IX

Kaprow, Allan
Born 1927 in Atlantic City; lives in Glen Head,
N.Y.
Pl. 340

Kasteel, Bart van
Born 1921 in Amsterdam; lives in Amsterdam

Katan, Roger
Born 1931 in Berguent, Morocco; lives in New
York.
1966 The New School of Social Research,
New York

Katz, Alex
Born 1927 in New York.
1960 and 1961 Stable Gallery, New York
1964, 1965 and 1967 Fischbach Gallery, New
York
1967 David Stuart Gallery, Los Angeles

Kelly, Elsworth
Born 1923 in Newburgh, N.Y.; lives in New
York.
1951 Galerie Arnaud, Paris
1956 Betty Parsons Gallery, New York
1965 Sidney Janis Gallery, New York

Kelly, J. Wallace
Lives in USA.
Pl. 243

Kienholz, Edward
Born 1927 in Fairfield, Washington; lives in
Los Angeles.
1964 Dwan Gallery, Los Angeles
1966 and 1967 Dwan Gallery, New York
1966 Los Angeles County Museum of Art
Pl. 14, 125, 127, 128, 129, 155, 156, 358, IV

King, Phillip
Born 1934 in Tunis; lives in London.
1964 Rowan Gallery, London
Pl. 218, 219, XI

King, William
Born 1925 in Florida; lives in New York.
Pl. 53

Kipp, Lyman
Born 1919 in Dobbs Ferry, N.Y.; lives in New
York.
1960, 1962, 1964 and 1965 Betty Parsons Gallery, New York

Klein, Yves
Born 1928 in Nice; died 1962 in Paris.
1956 Galerie Colette Allendy, Paris
1958 Galerie Iris Clert, Paris
1961 Museum Krefeld
1967 Jewish Museum, New York
Pl. 7, 359

Kolář, Jiří
Born 1914 in Protivin, Czechoslovakia; lives
in Prague.
1966 Galerie M. E. Thelen, Essen
Pl. 91

Kosice, G.
Born 1924 in Kosice, Hungary; lives in Paris.
1958 Galerie Denise René, Paris
1960 Drian Gallery, London
1965 Terry Dintenfass Gallery, New York

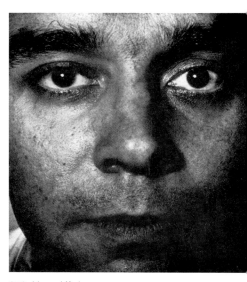

359 Yves Klein

360 Tetsumi Kudo

361 Yayoi Kusama, Lucio Fontana

362 Les Levine

363 Sol Lewitt

Kounellis, Jannis
Born 1936 in Athens; lives in Rome.
1967 Galleria l'Attico, Rome
Pl. 304, 305

Kowalski, Piotr
Born 1936 in Warsaw; lives in Montrouge.

Kricke, Norbert
Born 1922 in Düsseldorf; lives in Düsseldorf.
1954 Galerie Parnass, Wuppertal
1962 Museum Krefeld
Pl. 280

Kudo, Tetsumi
Born 1935 in Osaka; lives in Paris.
1966 Galerie M. E. Thelen, Essen
Pl. 44, 65, 126, 360, II

Kuehn, Gary
Born 1939 in Plainfield, N.J.
1965 and 1967 Bianchini Gallery, New York
Pl. 228

Kunst, Mauro
Lives in England.
Pl. 30

Kusama, Yayoi
Born in Nagano, Japan; lives in New York.
1966 Biennale Venice
1966 Galerie M. E. Thelen, Essen
Pl. 39, 113, 120, 133, 141, 334, 341, 342, 361, XII

Laing, Gerald
Born 1936 in Newcastle-on-Tyne; lives in New York and London.
1964 Institute of Contemporary Art, London

Lalanne, Claude
Lives in France.

Lalanne, F. X.
Lives in France.
Pl. 82, 85

Lardera, Berto
Born 1911 in La Spezia; lives in Paris.

Larrain, Gilles
Born 1938 in Dalat, Indochina; lives in New York.
1966 Southampton East Gallery, New York

Lassaw, Ibram
Born 1913 in Alexandria; lives in New York.

Latham, John
Born 1921 in Africa; lives in London.

Laurens, Henri
Born 1885 in Paris; died 1954 in Paris.
Pl. 239

Lenk, Kaspar-Thomas
Born 1933 in Berlin; lives in Stuttgart.
1959 Galerie Boukes, Wiesbaden
1966 Galerie Müller, Stuttgart
Pl. 256

Le Parc, Julio
Born 1928 in Mendoza, Argentina; lives in Paris.
1966 First Prize Biennale Venice
Pl. 251, 268, 270

Levi, Josef
Born 1938 in New York; lives in New York.
1966 Stable Gallery, New York

Levine, Les
Born 1936 in Dublin, Ireland; lives in New York.
1964 David Mirvish Gallery, Toronto
1964 Blue Barn Gallery, Ottawa
1966 Fischbach Gallery, New York
Pl. 162, 362

Lewitt, Sol
Born 1928 in Hartford, Conn.; lives in New York.
1967 Dwan Gallery, Los Angeles
Pl. 234, 235, 363

Liberman, Alexander
Born 1912 in Kiev; lives in New York.
1960, 1962, 1963 and 1964 Betty Parsons Gallery, New York
1965 Galleria dell'Ariete, Milan

Lijn, Liliane
Lives in Paris.
Pl. 279

Linder, Jean
Born 1938 in Berkeley, California; lives in New York.
1962 Oakland Art Museum, Oakland
1965 Graham Gallery, New York
1967 Graham Gallery, New York

Lipchitz, Jacques
Born 1891 in Druskieniki, Lithuania; lives in New York.

Lippold, Richard
Born 1915 in Milwaukee, Wisc.; lives in Trenton, N.J.

Lloyd, Tom
Born 1929; lives in New York.
1965/66 Art Turned On, Institute of Contemporary Art, Boston

Lombardo, Sergio
Born 1939 in Rome; lives in Rome.

Lopakov, Georgii Ivanovich
Born 1944 in Moscow; lives in St Tomilino, USSR.

Lo Savio, Francesco
Born 1935 in Rome; died 1963 in Marseilles.
1961 Museum Schloß Morsbroich, Leverkusen
Pl. 200, 364

Luginbühl, Bernard
Born 1929 in Bern; lives in Mooseedorf.

Lukin, Sven
Born 1934 in Riga; lives in New York.
1959 Nexus Gallery, Boston
1961 Betty Parsons Gallery, New York
1963 Dwan Gallery, Los Angeles

Lye, Len
Born 1901 in Christchurch, New Zealand; lives in New York.
1965 Albright-Knox-Gallery, Buffalo

Machlin, Sheldon
Born 1918.
1965/66 Art Turned On, Institute of Contemporary Art, Boston

Mack, Heinz
Born 1931 in Lollar; lives in Düsseldorf.
1957, 1958, 1960, 1965 Galerie Schmela Düsseldorf
1966 Howard Wise Gallery, New York
1967 Op Art Galerie, Esslingen

Malevich, Kasimir
Born 1878 in Kiev; died 1935 in Leningrad.

Malina, Frank
Born 1912 in Brenham, Texas; lives in Boulogne-sur-Marne, France.
1953 Galerie Henri Tronche, Paris
1954 Galerie Arnaud, Paris
1961 Galleria Schwarz, Milan

Mallary, Robert
Born 1917 in Toledo, Ohio; lives in New Rochelle, N.Y.
Pl. 140

Mallory, Ronald
Born 1935.
1965/66 Art Turned On, Institute of Contemporary Art, Boston

Manzoni, Piero
Born 1933 in Soncino; died 1963 in Milan.
1957 and 1958 Galleria Pater, Milan
1960 and 1961 Galerie Köpke, Copenhagen
1964 Galleria Schwarz, Milan
1967 Galerie M. E. Thelen, Essen
Pl. 41, 101, 291

Marchegiani, Elio
Born 1929 in Syracuse; lives in Rome.
1966 Galleria dell'Obelisco, Rome
Pl. 36, 37, 157

Mari, Enzo
Born 1932 in Novara.
1953 Galleria S. Fedele, Milan
1957 Galleria B 24, Milan
1959, 1961, 1963 and 1964 Galleria Danese, Milan
1963 Galleria Blu, Milan

Marini, Marino
Born 1901 in Pistoia; lives in Florence.
1952 Biennale Venice
1962 Retrospective in Zürich

Marisol (Escobar)
Born 1930 in Paris; lives in New York.
1958 Leo Castelli Gallery, New York
1962 and 1964 Stable Gallery, New York
1966 Sidney Janis Gallery, New York
1967 Hanover Gallery, London
Pl. 12, 13, 45

Marotta, Gino
Born 1935 in Campobasso; lives in Rome.
Pl. 111, 135, 339, 365, V

Martin, Kenneth
Born 1905 in Sheffield; lives in Hampstead.

Martinez, Christina
Born 1938 in Bahia Blanca, Argentina; lives in Paris.
1967 Galerie Claude Levin, Paris

Mason, John
Born 1927 in Madrid, Nebraska; lives in Los Angeles.
1967 Los Angeles County Museum of Art

Massironi, Manfredo
Born 1937; lives in Padua
Member of Group N

364 Francesco Lo Savio

365 Gino Marotta

66 David Medalla

67 Christian Megert

68 Neimann

Mastroianni, Umberto
Born 1910 in Fontana Liri; lives in Turin.

Matisse, Paul
Born 1933; lives in Cambridge, Mass.
1965/66 Art Turned On, Institute of Contemporary Art, Boston

Matkovic, Tina
Born 1943 in New York; lives in New York.
1966 Primary Structures, Jewish Museum, New York

Mattox, Charles
Born 1910 in Kansas; lives in Los Angeles.
1946 Felix Landau Gallery, Los Angeles
1965/66 Art Turned On, Institute of Contemporary Art, Boston

McClanahan, P.
Born 1933 in Charleston.
1966 Licht Kunst Licht, Museum Eindhoven

McCracken, John
Born 1934 in Berkeley, California; lives in Costa Mesa, California.
1965 and 1967 Nicholas Wilder Gallery, Los Angeles
Pl. 224

Meadows, Bernard
Born 1915 in Norwich, England; lives in London.
1947 and 1957 Gimpel Fils, London
1952 and 1964 Biennale Venice
1957 Biennale São Paulo

Medalla, David
Born 1942 in Manila; lives in London.
Pl. 299, 300, 366

Mefferd, Boyd
Born 1941 in St Louis, Missouri; lives in Whitewater, Wisconsin.
1967 Lights in Orbit, Howard Wise Gallery, New York

Megert, Christian
Born 1936 in Bern; lives in Bern.
1959 Galerie Kasper, Lausanne
1959 Galerie Köpke, Copenhagen
1963 Galerie d, Frankfurt
Pl. 255, 285, 367

Meier-Denninghoff, Brigitte
Born 1923 in Berlin; lives in Paris.
1962 Biennale Venice
1963 Marlborough Gallery, London
1963 Staempfli Gallery, New York

Miki, Tomio
Born 1937; lives in Tokyo.
1958 Kunugi Gallery, Tokyo
Pl. 66

Minujín, Marta
Born 1941 in Buenos Aires; lives in Buenos Aires.

Mirko (Basaldella)
Born 1910 in Udine; lives in Cambridge, Mass.

Moholy-Nagy, Laszlo
Born 1895 in Bacsborsod, Hungary; died 1946 in Chicago.
1937 Founded the New Bauhaus in Chicago.
1966 Licht Kunst Licht, Museum Eindhoven

Moore, Henry
Born 1898 in Castleford, Yorkshire; lives in Much Hadham, Hertfordshire.
1928 Warren Gallery, London
1948 Biennale Venice
1953 Biennale São Paulo
Pl. 1, 248, 249

Morellet, François
Born 1926 in Cholet; lives in Cholet

Morgan, Anthony
Born 1938.
1966 Indica Gallery, London

Morris, Robert
Born 1931 in Kansas City; lives in New York.
1957 and 1959 Dilexi Gallery, San Francisco
1963, 1964 and 1965 Green Gallery, New York
1964 Galerie Schmela, Düsseldorf
1966 Dwan Gallery, Los Angeles
Pl. 90, 201, 202, 221, 227

Motonaga, Sadamasa
Born 1922 in Iga, Japan; lives in Osaka.
1956 Hanging Water Environment
Pl. 292

Muehl, Otto
Lives in Vienna.
Pls. 40, 107, 108

Müller, Juana
Born 1911 in Santiago, Chile; lives in Paris.

Müller, Robert
Born 1920 in Zürich; lives in Paris.

Munari, Bruno
Born 1907 in Milan; lives in Milan.
1960 and 1965 Museum of Modern Art, Tokyo
Pl. 308

Murray, Robert
Born 1936 in Vancouver; lives in New York.
1965 and 1966 Betty Parsons Gallery, New York

Myer, Peter
Born 1934 in New York; lives in Las Vegas.
1967 Lights in Orbit, Howard Wise Gallery, New York

Myers, Forrest
Born 1941 in Long Beach, California; lives in New York.
1966 Primary Structures, Jewish Museum, New York

Nagel, Hans
Born 1926 in Frankfurt; lives in Ziegelhausen near Heidelberg.
1957 Kunstverein Hanover
1965 Kunsthalle Mannheim

Naumann, Bruce
Born 1941 in Fort Wayne; lives in San Francisco.
1966 Nicholas Wilder Gallery, Los Angeles

Negret, Edgar
Born 1920 in Popayan, Colombia; lives in Rome.
1950 Peridot Gallery, New York
1951 Galerie Arnaud, Paris
1959 David Herbert Gallery, New York
1962 Museo de Bellas Artes, Caracas
1966 Graham Gallery, New York
Pl. 189, 190

Neimann
Born 1931 in Warsaw; lives in Paris.
1967 Galerie Raymonde Cazenave, Paris
Pl. 368

Nepraś, Karel
Lives in Prague.
Pl. 49

Nevelson, Louise
Born 1900 in Kiev; lives in New York.
1960 Museum of Modern Art, New York
1967 Whitney Museum, New York
1967 Galerie Daniel Gerris, Paris
Pl. 263

Newman, Barnett
Born 1905 in New York; lives in New York.
1950 and 1951 Betty Parsons Gallery, New York
Pl. 171, 173

Newsome, Victor
Born 1935 in Leeds, England; lives in Hull.
1966 Grabowski Gallery, London

Nikos, Kesarlis
Born 1930 in Saloniki; lives in Paris.

Nivola, Constantino
Born 1911 in Orani, Sardinia; lives in New York.

Noguchi, Isamu
Born 1904 in Los Angeles; lives in New York.
1961, 1963, 1965 and 1967 Cordier and Eckstrom, New York
Pl. 167, 168

Novak, Giora
Born 1934; lives in New York.

Novros, David
Born 1941 in Los Angeles; lives in Los Angeles.
1967 Dwan Gallery, Los Angeles
Pl. 230

Nusberg, Lev Voldemarovich
Born 1937; lives in Moscow.

Ohashi, Yutaka
Born 1923 in Hiroshima; lives in New York.
1955 Margaret Brown Gallery, Boston
1961 White Museum, Cornell University
Pl. 282, 286, 287, 288

Oldenburg, Claes
Born 1929 in Stockholm; lives in New York.
1959 Judson Gallery, New York
1960 Reuben Gallery, New York
1962 Green Gallery, New York
1963 Dwan Gallery, Los Angeles
1964 and 1966 Sidney Janis Gallery, New York
1964 Galerie Ileana Sonnabend, Paris
1966 Moderna Museet, Stockholm
1966 Robert Fraser Gallery, London
1967 Museum of Contemporary Art, Chicago
Pl. 105, 106, 121, 370

Olitski, Jules
Born 1926 in Orel; lives in Shaftesbury, Vermont.
Pl. 194

Oppenheim, Méret
Born 1913 in Berlin; lives in New York.

Orfé, Barbara de
Born 1933 in Southend, England; lives in London.
1964 Institute of Contemporary Art, London

369 Niki de Saint Phalle

370 Claes Oldenburg

271 Pino Pascali

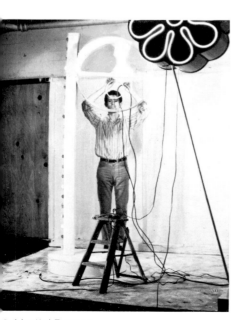

272 Martial Raysse

Padovano, Anthony
Born 1933; lives in North Bergen, N.J.
1962 Ruth White Gallery, New York

Paik, Nam June
Born 1932 in Seoul, Korea; lives in New York.
1963 Galerie Parnass, Wuppertal
1965 Bonino Galleria, New York
Pl. 320

Palatnik, Abraham
Born 1928 in Natal, Brazil; lives in Rio de Janeiro.
1960 Museo de Arte Moderna, Rio de Janeiro
1965 Howard Wise Gallery, New York
1965/66 Art Turned On, Institute of Contemporary Art, Boston

Pan, Marta
Born 1923 in Budapest; lives in Saint-Rémy-les-Chevreuse, France.

Paolozzi, Eduardo
Born 1924 in Edinburgh; lives in London.
1947 Mayor Gallery, London
1958 Hanover Gallery, London
1952 and 1960 Biennale Venice
1967 Hanover Gallery, London
Pl. 48, 193

Papa, Maria
Lives in Paris.
Pl. 55

Pascali, Pino
Born 1935 in Bari; lives in Rome.
1965 Galleria La Tartaruga, Rome
1966 Galleria Sperone, Turin
1967 Galerie M. E. Thelen, Essen
1967 Lo spazio dell'immagine, Foligno
Pl. 63, 76, 86, 87, 132, 137, 164, 272, 283, 301, 338, 371

Pasmore, Victor
Born 1908 in Chesham, England; lives in London.
1954 Institute of Contemporary Art, London

Peeters, Henk
Born 1925 in The Hague; lives in Arnhem.
1966 Licht Kunst Licht, Museum Eindhoven

Penalba, Alicia
Born 1918 in Argentina; lives in Paris.
1957 Galerie du Dragon, Paris
1964 Museum Schloß Morsbroich, Leverkusen

Pevsner, Antoine
Born 1887 in Orel, Russia; died 1962 in Paris
Pl. 241

Pfahler, Karl Georg
Born 1926 in Emetzheim; lives in Stuttgart.
1960 Galerie Müller, Stuttgart
Pl. 198

Phillips, Peter
Born 1939 in Birmingham; lives in Zürich and London.
1967 Galerie Bischofsberger, Zürich
Pl. VII

Picasso, Pablo
Born 1881 in Malaga; lives in the south of France.
Pl. 69, 70, 89

Piché, Roland
Born 1938 in London; lives in Essex

Piemonti, Lorenzo
Lives in Italy.
Pl. 192

Piene, Otto
Born 1928 in Laaspe, Westphalia; lives in Düsseldorf and New York.
1959, 1960, 1962, 1963 and 1966 Galerie Schmela, Düsseldorf
1962 Museum Schloß Morsbroich, Leverkusen
1965 Howard Wise Gallery, New York
Pl. 260

Pierelli, Attilio
Born 1924 in Sasso di Serra S. Quirico; lives in Rome.
1965 Galleria dell'Obelisco, Rome
Pl. 178, VI

Pinchbeck, Peter
Born 1931 in London; lives in New York.

Pistoletto, Michelangelo
Born 1933 in Biella; lives in Turin.
1964 Galerie Ileana Sonnabend, Paris
1966 Walker Art Center, Minneapolis
1967 Galerie Zwirner, Cologne
1967 Kornblee Gallery, New York
Pl. 110

Pomodoro, Arnaldo
Born 1926 in Morciano di Romagna; lives in Milan.

Pomodoro, Giò
Born 1930 in Orciano di Pesaro; lives in Milan.

Posenenske, Charlotte
Born 1930 in Wiesbaden; lives in Offenbach.
1967 Galerie h, Hanover
Pl. 199

Price, Kenneth
Born 1935 in Los Angeles; lives in Los Angeles.
1960, 1962 and 1964 Ferus Gallery, Los Angeles

Rabkin, L.
Born 1911 in Cincinnati.
1966 Licht Kunst Licht, Museum Eindhoven

Ramirez, Eduardo
Born 1923 in Pamplona, Colombia; lives in New York.
1960 David Herbert Gallery, New York
1964 Graham Gallery, New York
1964 Museo de Arte Moderno, Bogota
Pl. 188

Rauschenberg, Robert
Born 1925 in Port Arthur, Texas; lives in New York.
1960, 1961, 1963 Leo Castelli Gallery, New York
1963 The Jewish Museum, New York
1964 Whitechapel Art Gallery, London
1965 Walker Art Center, Minneapolis
Pl. 80, 83, 139

Ray, Man
Born 1890 in Philadelphia; lives in Paris.
1964 Galleria Schwarz, Milan
1966 Licht Kunst Licht, Museum Eindhoven

Raynaud, Jean-Pierre
Born 1939 in Bar-le-Duc; lives in Paris.
Pl. 159

Raysse, Martial
Born 1936 in Nice; lives in Nice.
1961 Galleria Schwarz, Milan
1962 Galerie Schmela, Düsseldorf
1962, 1964 Alexander Iolas Gallery, New York
1963, 1964 and 1967 Dwan Gallery, Los Angeles
1965 Stedelijk Museum, Amsterdam
Pl. 60, 109, 328, 329, 372

Remotti, Remo
Born 1924 in Rome; lives in Rome.

Richier, Germaine
Born 1904 in Grans; died 1959 in Montpellier.
1948 and 1952 Biennale Venice
1951 Biennale São Paulo
1958 World Fair, Brussels
Pl. 3

Richter, Vjenceslav
Born 1917; lives in Zagreb

Rickey, George
Born 1907 in South Bend, Indiana; lives in East Chatham, N.Y.
Pl. 196

Ridder, Willem de
Born 1939; lives in Amsterdam

Rivers, Larry
Born 1923 in New York; lives in New York

Romano, Salvator
Born 1925 in Cliffside Park, N.J.; lives in New York

Roszak, Theodore J.
Born 1907 in Poznan, Poland; lives in New York.
1959 Museum of Modern Art, New York
1960 Museum of Fine Arts, Baltimore
1960 Biennale Venice
Pl. 74

Ruscha, Edward
Born 1937 in Omaha, Nebraska; lives in Los Angeles

Saint-Phalle, Niki de
Born 1930 in Paris; lives in Paris.
1965 Galerie Alexandre Iolas, Paris
1966 Moderna Museet, Stockholm
Pl. 42, 43, 46, 369

Samaras, Lucas
Born 1936 in Kastoria, Greece; lives in New York.
1959 Reuben Gallery, New York
1961 and 1964 Green Gallery, New York
1964 Dwan Gallery, Los Angeles
1966 Pace Gallery, New York
Pl. 119, 343, 344

Sanderson, Christopher
Born 1939 in Jerusalem; lives in Leeds

Sandle, Michael
Born 1936 in Weymouth, Dorset; lives in Coventry.
1966 Grabowski Gallery, London
Pl. 100

Sanejouand
Lives in Paris.
Pl. 163

Santoro, Pasquale
Born 1933 in Ferrandina; lives in Rome.

373 Ernest Trova

374 Günter Uecker

375 Gregorio Vardanega

Wesselmann, Tom
Born 1931 in Cincinnati, Ohio; lives in New York.
Pl. 98

Westermann, H. C.
Born 1922 in Los Angeles; lives in Brookfield Center, Conn.
1959 and 1962 Allan Frumkin Gallery, Chicago
1961, 1963 and 1965 Allan Frumkin Gallery, New York
1962/63 Dilexi Gallery, Los Angeles and San Francisco
1966 Walker Art Center, Minneapolis
1966 Kansas City Art Institute
Pl. 92

Whitman, Robert
Born 1935; lives in New York.
1965/1966 Art Turned On, Institute of Contemporary Art, Boston

Willenbecher, John
Born 1936; lives in New York.
1965/66 Art Turned On, Institute of Contemporary Art, Boston

Wiley, William T.
Born 1937 in Bedford, Indiana; lives in Mill Valley, California.
1962 and 1964 Staempfli Gallery, New York

Witkin, Isaac
Born 1936 in Johannesburg, South Africa; lives in London.
1963 Rowan Gallery, London
1965 The New Generation, Whitechapel Art Gallery, London
1965 Biennale, Paris

Woodham, Derrick
Born 1940 in Blackburn; lives in London.
1965 The New Generation, Whitechapel Art Gallery, London
1966 Primary Structures, Jewish Museum, New York
Pl. 222

Wragg, John
lives in England.
1967 Galerie Alexandre Jolas, Paris
Pl. 207

Yaral
Born 1934 in Paris; lives in Arcueil

Zadkine, Ossip
Born 1890 in Smolensk; died 1967.
Pl. 238

Zammit, Norman
Born 1931 in Toronto; lives in Los Angeles

Zöllner, Waki
Born 1935 in Rattenberg; lives in Munich.
1967 Galerie M. E. Thelen, Essen
Pl. 317

Zurlo, Donald
Born 1934 in Trenton, New Jersey; lives in Allentown, N.J.
1967 Lights in Orbit, Howard Wise Gallery, New York
1967 Light Motion Space, Walker Art Center, Minneapolis

Acknowledgements

The following museums, galleries and collections have kindly provided photographs:

The Alan Gallery, New York 282, 286, 287, 288 – Galleria dell'Ariete, Milano 181 – Kunsthalle Basel 4 – Galerie Claude Bernard, Paris 17, 55, 56, 57, 58, 75 – Bianchini Gallery, New York 117, 228 – Galleria Bonino, New York 24, 84, 271, 320, 351 – Galerie Raymonde Cazenave, Paris 368 – Leo Castelli Gallery, New York 80, 83, 90, 131, 147, 148, 152, 153, 154, 172, 182, 201, 203, 204, 294 – Collection G. A. Baum, Wuppertal 118 – Collection Mr. J. A. Becht, Hilversum 44 – Collection Mr. and Mrs. Thomas Geismar, New York 232 – Collection Mrs. Kudo 126 – Collection Mrs. Pierre Matisse, New York 47 – Collection Mr. Henri Pierre Roché, Sèvres 165 – Collection Peter Stuyvesant Foundation 218 – Collection Time-Life Building, London 248, 249 – Collection Mr. and Mrs. Fred Weisman 171 – Collection Wilp, Düsseldorf 123 – Collection C. Bagley Wright 226 – Cordier & Eckstrom Gallery, New York 167, 168 – Daytons Gallery, Minneapolis, Minn. 185, 187, 302, 303 – Dwan Gallery, New York 125, 127, 128, 129, 142, 155, 156, 177, 202, 227, 229, 230, 231, 232, 234, 235 – Andre Emmerich Gallery, New York 215 – Richard Feigen Gallery, New York 215, 222, 223 – Fischbach Gallery, New York 160, 162, 208, 209, 210, 211, 292, 362 – Allan Frumkin Gallery, New York 92 – The Gallery of Modern Art, Including the Huntington Hartford Collection, New York 50 – Gimpel & Hanover Galerie, Zürich 143, 144 – Graham Gallery, New York 11, 188 – Green Gallery, New York 98, 326 – Hanover Gallery, London 6, 193, 207 – Sidney Janis Gallery, New York 8, 10, 12, 13, 18, 23, 45, 59, 116, 161, 346 – Indica Gallery, London 270, 279 – Galerie Alexander Iolas, Paris 7, 46, 82, 85, 328 – Alexander Iolas Gallery, New York 109, 186, 329 – Staatl. Amt für Denkmalpflege, Karlsruhe 68 – Kornblee Gallery, New York 61, 78, 130, 150, 325, 327 – Felix Landau Gallery, Los Angeles 16, 28, 29, 54, 179, 180 – Los Angeles County Museum of Art 14 – Galerie Müller, Stuttgart 191 – Galleria del Naviglio, Milano 336 – Galleria Notizie, Torino 41, 101, 291 – Galleria dell'Obelisco, Roma 36, 37 – Pace Gallery, New York 15, 99, 103, 112, 119, 134, 322, 323, 343, 344, 373 – Park Place Gallery, New York 146, 214, 233 – The Pasadena Museum, Pasadena 35 – Philadelphia Museum of Art, Philadelphia 71 – Stephen Radich Gallery, New York 104 – Galerie Denise René, Paris 268, 313, 314, 318, 319 – Rowan Gallery, London 217, 219 – Galleria La Salita, Roma 353 – Signals Gallery, London 265 – Stedelijk Museum, Amsterdam 133, 328 – Galleria Christian Stein, Torino 195, 225 – Alan Stone Gallery, New York 81, 95, 138, 140, 149 – Galeria Suvremene Umjenosti, Zagreb 258 – Galleria La Tartaruga 25, 26, 27, 62, 136, 352 – Vismara Arte Contemporanea, Milano 192, 367 – The Waddington Galleries, London 205, 206 – Walker Art Center, Eric Sutherland, Minneapolis 52 – Howard Wise Gallery, New York 308.

The following photographers and agencies have kindly provided photographs:

Archivo Amigos de Gaudi, Barcelona 122, 237 – The Associated Press, London 89 – Oliver Baker, New York 165 – Balz Burkhard, Bern 184, 367 – Serge Béguier 38 – Beuys-Wurmbach, Düsseldorf 118 – Ferdinand Boesch, New York 103, 263, 343, 344 – Harald Bookmann, Saarbrücken 261 – Maximilien Bruggmann, Lausanne 255 – Bob Bucknam 358 – Roman Buncék, Bratislava 309, 310, 316 – Casali-Domus 273 – Geoffrey Clements, New York 8, 10, 13, 18, 45, 53, 59, 90, 116, 216, 222, 223, 233, 286, 287, 288 – de Cordier, Montfermeil 268 – Hernan Diaz, Bogota 189, 190 – Augustin Dumage, Paris 85 – F. Engesser, Zürich 175 – David Farrel, Gloucester 72 – John A. Ferrari, Brooklyn 104, 186 – Sandra Flett, Chiswick 73 – Fotopress, Torino 164 – Paolo Gasparini, Caracas 246 – The Globe and Mail Library 347 – Hugh Gordon, London 100 – Norman Mc. Grath, New York 113, 141, 282 – C. M. J. de Groot, Otterlo 174 – Hans Hammarskiöld/Tio, Stockholm 42, 43, 80 – Howard Harrison Studio, New York 99, 112, 119, 134, 226, 322, 323, 354 – Nigel Hartnup, London 279 – T. C. Hartwell, Minneapolis 302, 303 – Lothar Heermann, Gelsenkirchen 335 – N. und C. Heinrich, Stuttgart 198 – Peter Heman, Basel 4 – Studio Yves Hervochon, Paris 318, 319 – Hofhaus Presse 123 – Jonathan Holstein, New York 173 – Kati Horne, Mexiko 274 – Errol Jackson, London 217, 219 – Pierre Joly-Véra Cardot, Paris 277 – Karbak, Roma 178 – Kim Lim 191 – Utz Klophaus, Wuppertal 348 – Ernst Knorr, Gelsenkirchen-Buer 253 – Karel Kublik, Praha 49, 91 – J. Masson, Paris 314 – Ministerio de Educacion, Venezuela 239, 247 – Peter Mögenburg, Leverkusen 259 – Peter Moore, New York 140, 320, 341, 351 – André Morain, Paris 105, 121, 370 – Ugo Mulas, Milano 181, 336 – Jon Naar, 373 – O. E. Nelson, New York 117, 228 – Gattin Nenad, Zagreb 258 – Atelier Neufert, Köln 260 – H. J. Orgler, London 197 – Clay Perry, London 299, 300 – Eric Pollitzer 98, 130, 161 Publifoto, Milano 361 – Nathan Rabin, New York 188, 271 – Reiner Rathenbeck, Düsseldorf 345 – Jan Ságl, Praha 266, 269 – Oscar Savio Roma 86, 87, 132 – John D. Schiff, New York 146, 155, 156, 196, 229, 234, 235, 308, 363 Schmölz & Ullrich, Köln 260 – Shunk Kender Paris 94, 176, 359 – Irena Sochorová, Bratislava 355 – Peter Stähli, Küsnacht 285 – Staub press, Zürich 143, 144 – Kok Storm, Amsterdam 257 – F. Tas, Antwerpen 93, 97 – Fran J. Thomas, Los Angeles 31, 33 – Charles Uht New York, 150 – Universal Photo Service, London 114 – Marc Vaux, Paris 159 – Walther Gorinchem 183 – John Webb FRPS, London 193 – Guy Weill 357 – K. Wetschaar, Amsterdam 356.

The following galleries and private individuals have generously provided colour reproductions:

Galerie Bischofberger, Zürich VII, IX – Dwan Gallery, Los Angeles IV – Tetsumi Kudo II Yayoi Kusama XII – Gino Marotta V – Galleria dell'Obelisco, Roma VI – Park Place Gallery, New York VIII – Rowan Gallery, London XI Galerie Thelen, Essen X.

Bibliography

1927–1954

K. Malewitsch: Die gegenstandslose Welt, München, 1927.

L. Moholy-Nagy: Vom Material zur Architektur, München, 1929.

J. Hudnut: Modern Sculpture, New York, 1929.

W. Pach: Duchamp-Villon, Formes 15, 1931.

H. Maryon: Modern Sculpture, London, 1933.

P. Fierens: Sculpteurs d'Aujourd'hui, Paris, 1933.

H. Read: Henry Moore, London, 1934.

R. H. Wilenski: The Meaning of Modern Sculpture, New York, 1935.

A. Barr: Cubism and Abstract Art, New York, 1936.

A. Hoff: Wilhelm Lehmbruck, Berlin, 1936.

C. Giedion-Welcker: Moderne Plastik, Zürich, 1937.

J. Rewald: Maillol, London, 1939.

J. J. Sweeney: Picasso and Iberian Sculpture, The Art Bulletin 23, 1941.

W. R. Valentiner: Origins of Modern Sculpture, New York, 1946.

B. Adriani: Probleme des Bildhauers, Ulm, 1948.

G. C. Argan: Henry Moore, Torino, 1948.

C. Giedion-Welcker: Schwitters or the Allusions of the Imagination, Magazine of Art, October 1948.

W. R. Valentiner: Sculpture by David Smith, Arts and Architecture, August, 1948.

C. Greenberg: The New Sculpture, Partisan Review 16, 1949.

M. Seuphor: L'Art Abstrait, Paris, 1949.

C. Seymour: Tradition and Experiment in Modern Sculpture, Washington, D.C., 1949.

J. A. Goris: Modern Sculpture in Belgium, Bruxelles, 1952.

A. C. Ritchie: Sculpture of the Twentieth Century, New York, 1952.

J. Struppeck: The Creation of Sculpture, New York, 1952.

M. Tapié: Un art autre, Paris, 1952.

L. Alloway: Britain's New Iron Age, Art News, 5, 1953.

U. Gertz: Plastik der Gegenwart, Berlin, 1953.

W. Hofmann: Vorbild und Abbild, Das Kunstwerk, 1953

G. Marchiori: Scultura Italiana Moderna, Venezia, 1953.

M. Middleton: Huit sculpteurs britanniques, Art d'Aujourd'hui, 3, 1953.

H. Pierce: Die letzte Lebenszeit von Kurt Schwitters, Das Kunstwerk, 1953.

E. H. Ramsden: Sculpture, Theme and Variations, London, 1953.

F. Adama von Scheltema: Vorzeitliche und moderne Plastik, Das Kunstwerk, 1953.

L. Alloway: Nine Abstract Artists, London, 1954.

R. Richman, Edit.: The Arts at Mid-Century, New York, 1954.

E. Trier: Moderne Plastik, Berlin, 1954.

1955

R. Banham: The New Brutalism, The Architectural Review 118.

A. M. Hammacher: Beeldhouwkunst van deze eeuw, Amsterdam.

C. Giedion-Welcker: Plastik des 20. Jahrhunderts, Stuttgart.

M. Joray: Schweizer Plastik der Gegenwart, Neuchâtel.

U. Kultermann: Arbeiten von Henry Moore für das Time/Life-Gebäude in London, Das Kunstwerk.

A. C. Ritchie: The New Decade, New York.

H. Schaefer-Simmern: Sculpture in Europe Today, Los Angeles.

1956

L. Alloway: Eduardo Paolozzi, Architectural Design, 4.

U. Kultermann: Café Voltaire, Augenblick, 2/3.

U. Kultermann: Brancusi, der Vater der modernen Skulptur, baukunst und werkform 3.

U. Kultermann: Reg Butler, Kroniek van Kunst en Kultuur 5/6.

U. Kultermann: Germaine Richier, Schweizer Rundschau, 11.

H. Read: The Art of Sculpture, London.

1957

H. Griffin: Auriga, Andromeda, Cameoleopardalis, Art News, 12.

U. Kultermann: Julio Gonzales, baukunst und werkform, 7.

U. Kultermann: Raummagie in der Skulptur. Zu den Werken von Berto Lardera, baukunst und werkform, 10.

H. Platte: Plastik. Die Kunst des 20. Jahrhunderts, II, München.

1958

W. Hofmann: Die Plastik des 20. Jahrhunderts, Frankfurt.

U. Kultermann: Das Denkmal in unserer Zeit, Das Kunstwerk, 11/12.

I. Sandler: La sculpture américaine, Aujourd'hui, 9.

1959

E.C.Goossen: The End of the Object, Art International.
U.Kultermann: Englische Plastik der Gegenwart, Das Kunstwerk, 1.
U.Kultermann: Suggestivität des Materials-moebel und decoration, 3.
U.Kultermann: Der Bildhauer Norbert Kricke, moebel und decoration, 8.
E.Newman: Masterpieces of European Sculpture, New York, 1959, 1961.
A. Moles: L'oeuvre de Pomodoro, Art International.
P.Restany: Julio Gonzales, Art International.
P.Restany: L'autre Calder, Art International.
P.Restany: César le ferrailleur, Art International.
M.Seuphor: Die Plastik unseres Jahrhunderts, Köln.
E.C.Goossen: The Plastic Poetry of Joseph Cornell, Art International 1959/1960.
P.Selz: New Images of Man, New York.

1960

L.Alloway: Paolozzi and the comedy of waste, Cimaise, 7.
P.-M.Grand: Giacometti, Art News.
U.Kultermann: Brigitte Meier-Denninghoff, Junge Künstler 1960/1961, Köln.

1961

C.Greenberg: Art and Culture, Boston.
H.Janis and R.Blesh: Collage, New York.
U.Kultermann: Berto Lardera, Das Kunstwerk, 10.
P.Restany: Die Beseelung des Objekts, Das Kunstwerk, 7/8.
W.C.Seitz: The Art of Assemblage, New York.

1962

B.Alfieri: Jorge Eielson, Metro, 8.
D.Ashton: Illusion and Fantasy, Lee, Metro, 8.
M. Bonicatti: Gianfranco Baruchello, Metro, 8.
R.Freeman: Painted Sculpture by Anthony Caro, Metro, 6.
A.Jouffroy: Crippa, Paris.
A.Jouffroy: Hiquely, Paris.
U.Kultermann: Farbe als räumliche Modulation, Speculum Artis, 1/2.
U.Kultermann: Norbert Kricke, deutsche bauzeitung, 9.
R.Maillard: A Dictionary of Modern Sculpture, London.
J.Reichardt: Paolozzi, Metro, 8.
T.Sauvage: Art Nuclaire, Paris.

E.Trier: Notizen zum neuen Denkmal, Der Mensch und die Künste, Festschrift für Heinrich Lützeler zum 60. Geburtstag. Düsseldorf.
H.Wescher: Die neuen Realisten und ihre Vorläufer, Werk.

1963

L.Alloway: Sculpture as a Cliché, Artforum, 10.
J.Coplans: Charles Mattox. Three Machines, Artforum, 1.
M.Fried: Anthony Caro, Art International, 7.
P.Jones: Arman and the Power of Objects, Art International, 3.
U.Kultermann: Junge deutsche Bildhauer, Mainz.
H.Ladendorf: Denkmäler und Mahnmale seit 1945, Monumenta Judaica, Köln.
G.Marchiori: Modern French Sculpture, New York.
M.Ragon: Naissance d'un art nouveau, Paris.
J.Reichardt: Pop Art and After, Art International, 2.
P.Restany: The New Realism, Art in America, 1.
B. Rose: Dada then and now, Art International, 1.
B. Rose: Americans 1963, Art International, 7.
J.Selz: Modern Sculpture. Origins and Evolution, New York.

1964

P.Blake: God's Own Junkyard, New York.
W.Hopps: Boxes, Art International, 3.
A.Jouffroy: Une révolution du regard, Paris.
U.Kultermann: Bildende Kunst og Arkitektur – en ny enhet, Byggekunst, 6.
U.Kultermann: Jóvenes escultoras alemanas, Humboldt, 20.
N.Lynton: Latest Developments in British Sculpture, Art and Literature Summer.
H.Read: A Concise History of Modern Sculpture, London.
J.Reichardt: Caro and the envivonmental sculpture, Architectural Design, 10.
J.Reichardt: The Revival of Machine Esthetic, Architectural Design, 10.
H.Richter: Dada-Kunst und Antikunst, Köln.
A.R.Solomon: The New American Art, Art International, 3.

1965

M.Amaya: Pop As Art, London.
G.C.Argan: Jochen Hiltmann, Art International, 5.
G.Baro: Britain's New Sculpture, Art International, 6.

G. Baro: Britain's Young Sculptors, arts magazine, 12.

A. Bowness: Modern Sculpture, London.

J. R. Brest: Letter from Buenos Aires, Art International.

J. Claus: Kunst heute, Reinbek.

J. Coplans: The New Abstraction on the West Coast, Studio International, 5.

J. Coplans: Phillip King, Studio International, 12.

R. G. Dienst: Pop Art, Wiesbaden.

A. Eliot: Art in Israel, Art in America, 10/11.

A. Forge: Some New British Sculptors, Artforum, 5.

O. Hahn: Christo's Packages, Art International, 4.

H. Hopkins: Edward Kienholz; Art in America, 10/11.

D. Judd: Specific Object, Arts Yearbook, 8.

V. Horvat Pintaric: Spazio e cronolumino-dinamismo di Nicola Schöffer, La Biennale di Venezia 57/58.

M. Kozloff: The Further Adventures of American Sculpture, arts magazine, 2.

U. Kultermann: Kunst und Leben in neuer Einheit, Speculum Artis, 2.

U. Kultermann: Pop und Hap, die realisierte Dynamik in der zeitgenössischen Kunst, Speculum Artis, 3.

U. Kultermann: The New Work of Kaspar-Thomas Lenk, Art International, 5.

R. Manvell: Tajiri, Art International.

J. Reichardt: Color in Sculpture, Quadrum, 18.

J. Reichardt: Satire in Art, Architectural Design, 12.

P. Restany: Buenos Ayres et le Nouvel Humanisme, domus, 4.

P. Restany: Yves Klein et son mythe, Quadrum, 18.

P. Restany: Claes Oldenburg, Metro 9.

R. Richetin: Le Pop Art et l'artiste, Paris.

G. Rickey: Scandale de Succès, Art International, 5.

G. Rickey: Kinesis Continued, Art in America, 12/1 65/66.

B. Rose: Looking at American Sculpture, Artforum, 2.

B. Rose: ABC Art, Art in America, 10.

J. Rublowski und K. Heyman: Pop Art, New York.

I. Sandler: The New Cool Art, Art in America, 1.

E. Spaeth: Leningrad-Moscow-Kiew, Art in America, 12/1 65/66.

A. S. Weller: Contemporary American Painting and Sculpture, Urbana.

F. S. Wight: Edward Kienholz, Art in America, 10/11.

1966

J.–C. Ammann: Jean Tinguely, werk 3.

J.–C. Ammann: Das Problem des Raumes im Werk Alberto Giacomettis, werk 6.

J. Barnitz: A Latin Answer to Pop, arts magazine, 6.

O. Carlisle: A Soviet Sculptor, Ernst Neizvestni, Art in America, 1/2.

A. Cortesi: Joseph Cornell, Artforum, 4.

J. Coplans: Five Los Angeles Sculptors at Irvine, Artforum, 2.

R. G. Dienst: Drei Aspekte der neuen englischen Plastik, Das Kunstwerk, 3.

A. Forge: Interview with Anthony Caro, Studio International, 1.

H. Geldzahler: George Segal, Quadrum 19.

H. A. Giusti: Primary Structures at Jewish Museum, D'Ars Agency, 3–4.

A. Goldin: The Sculpture of George Sugarman, arts magazine, 6.

B. Johnston: Living Things For What They Are. New York by Les Levine, Artforum, 3.

A. Jouffroy: Jean Tinguely, L'Oeuil, 4.

A. Jouffroy: Les Objecteurs, Quadrum 19.

A. Kaprow: Assemblage, Environments and Happenings, New York.

U. Kultermann: Die Sprache des Schweigens, Quadrum 20.

U. Kultermann: Besuch bei Joseph Cornell, Die Tat, 17. 12. 66.

L. Lippard: Pop Art, New York.

M. McLuhan: Understanding Media: The Extensions of Men, New York.

R. Morris: Notes on Sculpture, Artforum, 2.

C. Oldenburg: Extract from the Studio Notes, Artforum, 1.

N. Ponente: Continuità di Fontana, La Biennale di Venezia 60.

J. Reichardt: The Falling Man, Architectural Design.

P. Restany: Argentina d'oggi, D'Ars Agency, 1/2.

D. Robbins: Recent Still-Life, Art in America, 1/2.

H. Rosenstein: Ideologue in Lotosland, Art News, 10.

I. H. Sandler: Sugarman Makes a Sculpture, Art News, 5.

B. Smith: Art in Motion, Canadian Art, 1.

B. Smith: Jim Dine, Canadian Art, 1.

R. Smithson: Entropy and the New Monuments, Artforum, 6.

Y. Tono: New Talent in Tokyo, Art in America, 2.

S. Tillim: The Underground Pre-Raphaelitism of Edward Kienholz, Artforum, 8.

M. Tuchman: A Decade of Edward Kienholz, Artforum, 8.

D. Waldman: Samaras. Reliquaries for St. Sade, Art News, 10.

1967

E. Abeel: Armory '66, arts magazine, 3.
D. Adrian: Edward Higgins, Artforum, 1.
D. Adrian: Walter de Maria, Artforum, 1.
L. Alloway: Art in Escalation, arts magazine, 3.
J.–C. Ammann: Martial Raysse, Du, 4.
G. Baro: Alexander Liberman. Art as Involvement, Art International, 3.
J. Coplans: An Interview with Kenneth Snelson, Artforum, 3.
M. Fried: New York by Anthony Caro, Artforum, 2.
M. Fried: Ronald Davis, Artforum, 4.
S. Geist: Brancusi, Artforum, 3.
C. Finch: Jann Hawarth and Nicholas Munro, Art International, 1.
C. Greenberg: Recentness of Sculpture, Art International, 4.
A. M. Hannacher: Modern French Sculpture, London.
A. M. Hammacher: Modern English Sculpture, London.
J. P. Hodin: Anthony Caro, Quadrum, 20.
R. Hunt: Yves Klein, Artforum, 1.
P. Leider: John Chamberlain, Artforum, 2.
L. R. Lippard: Max Ernst and a Sculpture of Fantasy, Art International, 3.
L. R. Lippard: Perverse Perspectives, Art International, 3.
L. R. Lippard: Ronald Bladen's „Black Triangle", Artforum, 3.
K. McShine: More than Black, arts magazine, 3.
H. Paris: Sweet Land of Funk, Art in America, 4.
B. Rose: The Value of Didactic Art, Artforum, 4.
S. Scarpitta: Backyard Racers, arts magazine 3.
Y. Tono: Japan, Artforum, 4.